To: *Music and Children*
with love ! !

reflections for parents and teachers

A. Ramón Rivera and Thelma Gruenbaum

To: Music and Children with love!!

(Reflections for Parents and Teachers)

Copyright © 1979 A. Ramón Rivera
and Thelma Gruenbaum

1st Printing September 1979

Publisher: exPressAll
P. O. Box 427
Brookline, Massachusetts 02146

In this

INTERNATIONAL YEAR OF THE CHILD

we dedicate this book

to all the children who have taught us so much
and
to our parents who gave us the gift of music

ACKNOWLEDGMENTS

We are deeply grateful for
helpful suggestions on the manuscript to:

JEAN STACKHOUSE, piano teacher and pedagogical teacher at the New England Conservatory of Music

JEAN ALDERMAN, the first pedagogical teacher of Mr. Rivera at the New England Conservatory of Music

FANNIE YUTAN, Past President of the Morning Etude in Springfield, Illinois

MICHAEL GRUENBAUM, for his encouragement, friendship and assistance in the preparation of the manuscript

DAVID, PETER and LEON GRUENBAUM, for practical advice on wind instruments, jazz and popular music

and

ROBERT TREANOR, for cover design

Boston, Massachusetts   A. Ramón Rivera
September 1979   Thelma Gruenbaum

CONTENTS

Appendix

FOREWORD

The general education and schooling of children is, on the whole, quite well prescribed for parents, but when it comes to music there is a dilemma which the average parent has no ability to handle. Whether or not the child is musically gifted (and most children are in one degree or another), a knowledge of and acquaintance with music can enhance the quality of his future life.

This book, so exhaustively and intelligently written by two dedicated teachers, is a long-awaited answer to parents' and teachers' questions and concerns about the musical education of their children.

After working with young people for many years, I am convinced that we have here in the United States a wealth of talent and musical potential among our young people waiting to be tapped.

Bravo for this book which will go far in accomplishing this purpose.

Harry Ellis Dickson

(Mr. Dickson is the Assistant Director of the Boston Pops Orchestra, 1st violinist with the Boston Symphony, and Music Director of Boston Symphony Youth Concerts.)

PRELUDE

Music has become an integral part of children's lives because of easy access to quality recordings and concerts. Also, they hear music on television, the radio, the movies, in the supermarket and in the dentist's chair! By the time children reach school age, they have heard thousands of hours of music.

We believe that children should gain an appreciation of music, and develop some musical skills through instruction rather than learning about music passively through listening to records, the radio, watching television and attending concerts.

Music should be taught so that each individual's needs are met. Music is a special gift with a place in the life of every child, even though that place may differ from one child to another. The teaching and learning of music, therefore, must be adapted and shaped to reach all - the average, the gifted, or the special needs child. We advocate music lessons that will help each individual develop his full musical potential.

In the United States, the process of learning music is neither considered to be every child's "birthright" nor is a widespread effort made to search for and train those children who demonstrate musical talents. Instead, the teaching of music in the schools varies widely depending on locale with much of the responsibility for music lessons thrust onto the parents. By providing information on many aspects of music instruction and education, we feel we can help parents and music teachers make informed decisions for every child.

We bring to the writing of this book a special interest in music for each individual child. We feel uniquely qualified to write about music and children because of our backgrounds. One author is a trained musician, music teacher, educator, and performer with many years of experience; the other author is trained as a research psychologist, educator, and is the parent of teenaged musicians. We bring to this task an understanding of children and their development, a firm conviction of the importance of professionalism in the teaching of music, and an awareness of pedagogical research and methods.

The writing of this book required an extensive search through the literature, numerous discussions with other musicians and parents, and an examination of our own experiences and knowledge. From this project we gained many insights into how to help children with music as well as some reflections on the current state and future of music education.

MUSIC EDUCATION BEFORE FORMAL LESSONS

Most people believe that music lessons should not start before the child is six years old and many parents and teachers wait until the child is nine years old. It is never too early to expose the child to good music. In fact, there are some music education programs designed for preschool children.

From the moment a child is born, he can respond to music. Studies have shown that young babies can learn to recognize different musical compositions after repeated hearings. A parent can and should expose the child to good music from many sources .... the radio, tape recorder, phonograph records, and live music. The mother and father should sing to the child from the time he is a baby. Also, children can attend concerts at an early age: good outdoor concerts, performances given by children at local schools or music schools, and an occasional professional performance. Violinist Yehudi Menuhin's parents took him to classical concerts from the age of two because they could not afford a babysitter. This undoubtedly enhanced his early love for, and interest in, music. Recently, James Levine, conductor of the Metropolitan Opera Orchestra, explained to the television audience that when he was eight years old he was in a production of Smetana's "Bartered Bride". Many years later he urged the Met to stage a new production of that opera. The production, televised and seen by millions of viewers, reached and may have influenced many young viewers.

In addition to listening to music and singing (responsibilities which can be handled by the parents), the next step in a child's musical education will depend on the musical resources of the community. If there is a nursery school available where music and the arts are incorporated into the curriculum, this might be a good choice. A better choice is a special class for young children which focuses on music and movement. The class might be organized according to the principles of Jacques-Dalcroze, Orff, Suzuki or Kodály.

Eurhythmics

Eurhythmics, first devised by Jacques-Dalcroze, is based upon the concept that music and movement are inseparable and that the body is a natural instrument for the study of rhythm. Since all animation of the body - heart beat, pulse and breathing - is rhythmic, Dalcroze believed that "musical theory is too often the study of signs of music, instead of being the experience and analysis of music itself." In a Dalcroze class, the children "become" the music.

A typical eurhythmics class, composed of four and five year olds, is involved with the coordination of simple, improvised bodily movements made with musical rhythms as a means of self-expression. The teacher helps the children develop an understanding of basic musical concepts through movement to music. This works with young children because the teaching is adapted to a child's way of thinking and learning. The French psychologist Jean Piaget describes this learning process in the following way: "to know something is not merely to be told it or to see it, but to act upon it."

The learning process is best explained by an example. To explain the musical concepts of "crescendo" and "diminuendo" one of the authors does the following: "I tell the class to become tiny little seeds. Without explanation, the children get down on the floor and curl up their bodies into little balls. I go to the piano and begin to play, explaining that they are to act out what the music tells them to do. At first I play softly and then gradually I increase the volume and texture of my improvisation. The children slowly uncurl and gradually get up, until they are standing tall (crescendo). At this point, I can bring other musical concepts into the exercise: for example, the branches of the tree swaying in the wind (3/4 tempo). Then I have them act out different tempi

and dynamics through the leaves (by finger movements).
Next I explain that autumn has arrived and leaves drop
down to the ground (diminuendo). After this, I let the
children suggest other ideas for the same principle...
chickens hatching from eggs, cakes rising in the oven,
etc. - and we act them out."

How much more meaningful the ideas become when
the child experiences the concept! Think of the child
whose teacher shows him a printed page with the following examples:

      crescendo   diminuendo

and says, "when you see the sign on the left, you play
louder and when you see the sign on the right, you play
softer."

We can sum up the learning process this way. When
the child hears the music, he curls up or stands tall
(a physical response to the musical environment). After making these movements, the child understands the
principle involved so that he can apply it to other
examples....hatching of chickens, cakes rising in the
oven, etc. After that, the child can abstract the
concept and sum it up in a word: "crescendo", "diminuendo", etc. Through movement to music, it is possible to teach children other musical concepts: rhythm,
the scales, intervals, time signatures, etc.

Not every parent accepts this approach to music.
One parent whose child attended a eurhythmics class
told the teacher that the child could barely wait for
Saturday mornings. The mother had been observing the
class through the glass windows and could see why the
class was so much fun...the children removed their
shoes, ran and jumped in that vast space. But, she won-
dered, was her child really learning anything about
music?

Perhaps she expected the child to bring home
"proofs" of what he was learning musically. She miss-

ed the point, just as parents who pick up their children from nursery school err in asking the child "what did you make today?" rather than "what did you do?" (They are emphasizing a "product" rather than the "process" of learning.) What this mother did not comprehend was that the boy was coming to an institution filled with music (it happened to be the New England Conservatory of Music), that he really enjoyed the class, that he was under the tutelage of a musician, that he was moving to music, that he met his "musical" peers in the class and that he was learning about music because the activity covered the principles and the organized symbols of music that he would accept later with intelligence, ease and experience.

Children who have begun their musical education with eurhythmics have an advantage. When they play their instruments, even the printed pauses are musically meaningful. This early training encourages a natural facility in the playing which is very attractive to the listener. They seem to have a familiarity, knowledge and control of the instrument that enhances the performance, almost as if the instrument were an extension of themselves.

Orff

Another music education program which may be available in the community is the Orff method. It is based on the idea that feeling comes before understanding. Rhythm, in speech and movement, is used to explore music. Orff music education starts with the rhythmic pattern of one word, followed by two, and gradually becomes more complicated. Moving on to melody, the music experience starts with chants of childhood (a falling minor third), and then adds tones of the pentatonic scale, followed by the major and minor scales.

To explain note values, rhythm, phrases, etc.,the Orff method uses speech, children's rhymes, proverbs, etc. There is a special set of Orff instruments which are used - melodic instruments (glockenspiels, xylophones, and metallophones - with soprano, alto and bass pitches). Each bar of the xylophone has a name of a note engraved on it. Bars are removable so that different patterns of tones can be played. (Part of the appeal of the Orff method is that children can produce pleasing harmonies instantly through imaginative orchestration.) Since the percussion instruments are of professional quality and are expensive, soprano and alto recorders are used frequently in Orff instruction. Also, drums (tuned to a definite pitch) and simple stringed instruments (guitar, cello, etc. which can be plucked or bowed) are used. Other instruments include: tambourines, triangles, woodblocks, cymbals, rattles, and jingle bells.

Kodály

The Kodály music education method stresses reading and writing of music as part of its goal. The Kodály method originated in Hungary and is based primarily on singing. Kodály believed that the best approach to music is through the instrument most accessible to everyone - the human voice. Music is introduced in nursery school through folk songs and nursery rhymes. The child learns about rhythm by stepping and walking to music. The child also claps to music. Kodály has a system of hand signals which help the child see the height or depth of a sound they hear (the pitch). Children are taught a system of sol-fa, naming the intervals of the scale.

Kodály described his method this way: "At the beginning, the aim is to equip the pupil with such a mastery of music that he is able to transpose the visual image of the score almost automatically into sound that he can sing; and at the same time to transcribe on paper the sounds that he hears." In other words, his system stresses the learning of sightsinging and the development of the ability to listen to music and write it down (dictation).

In Kodaly's method the first note of any given scale is called "do" (or tonic). This is the moveable "do" system which has caused debate among musicians, particularly those who prefer the fixed "do". In the fixed "do" system, the syllables are invariably applied to the notes of the C major scale. As an example, the first three notes of "Mary Had a Little Lamb" in the key of E Major would be G sharp,F sharp, E. Musicians who favor moveable "do" would sing "mi-re-do" while musicians favoring fixed "do" would call the notes "sol-fa-mi". One of the arguments advanced by musicians who favor fixed "do" is that contemporary music has no tonic or first degree of the scale or key signatures so that a moveable "do" is not appropriate. However, what we really want to develop is the ability to look at the printed page and translate it into sound using our experience of the musical interval.To achieve this, training by either the fixed or moveable "do" method can be used, provided the child has been correctly instructed by the teacher.

Suzuki

Another teaching system that began in Japan and has been adapted for use in America is the Suzuki Method. Originally developed to teach violin to youngsters beginning at age three, it has since expanded to include the teaching of piano, cello, flute, art, etc. The basic philosophy underlying the Suzuki method is that all children (unless they have physical defects that specifically prevent them from learning) do learn to speak a language and can also learn to perform music. In the Suzuki method, it is firmly believed that education and environment have far greater impact than inborn ability or talent. The ear for music, according to Suzuki, can be developed by listening to good music. Music is taught by rote (by ear) with the help of the mother who attends classes along with the child, listens to what happens and then takes over the responsibility of helping the child practice at home throughout the week, reinforcing what the child was taught in class. Learning is begun at a very early age and each step is thoroughly mastered before taking the next step. While recognizing that there are individual differences so that some children progress faster than others, the Suzuki method allows each child to progress at his own rate. For example, one child needed to spend two years working on music at the level of "Twinkle, Twinkle, Little Star", but he finally mastered it and then went on to a higher level.

Musical notation is introduced at a later stage. Suzuki teachers believe that testing for musical aptitude is meaningless because students who do not do well at first often surprise the teacher by doing well later.

Although the preceding philosophies and music education methods have much to commend them, they are useless for the parent who lives in a community which has no classes. In that case, the parent will have to rely on his resources by providing some early musical experiences at home. Although the task sounds formidable, if love for music is expressed in the home, then half the battle is won!

Home-based Music Education

When her first child was small, one of the authors was unable to locate a euthythmics class for him. She decided to use her training as a nursery school teacher by providing musical experiences at home. Mother and child began by listening to many records, including classical and folk music. After hearing the folk songs, the mother sang them and encouraged the child to sing, too. Folk songs were accompanied by playing simple chords on a guitar. At the library, they found collections of folk songs, Mother Goose rhymes and nursery rhymes. Eventually, the purchase of a second-hand piano provided another source of accompaniment.

Along with folk singing and listening to records, the mother taught the child some finger games she had

learned from nursery school teaching ("The Eensy Ween-
sy Spider"), movement games ("London Bridge", "Punchi-
nello", "the Hoky Poky"), all using singing and movement. Simple Mother Goose rhymes were adapted for
marching (e.g. "The King of France")."Hot Cross Buns"
was a good song for clapping. Songs and music encouraged and were used to accompany fast and slow movement. "Musical Chairs" taught the child to listen
carefully for silence when the music stopped.The mother made up songs to accompany action or sometimes she
sang old songs such as "Here we go Round the Mulberry
Bush". The child was encouraged to make up his own
songs and words.

    Realizing that children enjoy experimenting and
making sounds, and also listening to sounds, she went
to the public library for records on natural sounds
and sound effects. At home a percussion section was
developed: pots, pans, and boxes tapped by wooden
spoons. Dried beans in a coffee can were used as a
rattle. An inner tube stretched across a coffee can
became a drum. A board with nails set at various intervals, and then stretched with rubber bands, served
as a "guitar" and provided an opportunity to experi-
ment and learn about the relationship of string length
to pitch. After the child had learned to discriminate
pitches, the author used water glasses, encouraging
the child to fill them to different heights. The child
learned to depend on his ears to determine how much to
fill the glasses, and then to produce a scale on which
he could play tunes. Since the child had a keen sense
of pitch, he was able to collect a series of coke and
soda bottles, tune them precisely, then produce eerie
tones by blowing across the tops. One other experience which fostered the boy's musical interest was
attendance at a weekly tap dancing lesson. Although
he never became a skilled dancer, this experience improved his sense of rhythm and today he is quite grace-
ful on the tennis court.

    Although the home-based experiences do not com-
pletely replace any of the musical education systems

described here, they still serve the purpose of interesting preschoolers in music, participating in, and thinking about, rhythm and movement, singing,and sound itself - all good prerequisites for further music study.

In summary, if preschool classes are unavailable in your community, there is still a great deal that a parent can do. The years before the age of five are both precious and formative. Prime opportunities for learning and development are lost if nothing is done in those early years. It is important to realize,too, that the musical experiences are enjoyable for the parent as well as the child. The child probably won't even be aware of the fact that he is learning or being taught. And the parent gets a chance to do something of real value with the child.

The parent who has investigated available preschool musical activities and/or exposed his child at home or in the community to musical experiences will have a good idea of the child's interest in or capacity to learn music. At this point, it is probably time to begin thinking of the next step, formal music lessons.

The parent should analyze his or her <u>motivation</u>, asking herself,"why do I want to give my child music lessons?" An honest and thorough examination of the reasons often proves helpful if undertaken <u>before</u> lessons are started. Many of the reasons for providing lessons to the child are the wrong ones. Since music lessons are expensive in terms of time and money, as well as in personal anguish (if things do not go well), it is important to think things through <u>before</u> the child is signed up with a teacher.

Signs of Music Readiness

A parent may have noticed that the child moves to music, conducts along with the Boston Pops on television, or mimics the playing of an instrument when he hears music. The parent should recognize that such behavior is normal and only provides clues as to whether the child might have a good ear, be rhythmical, and be well-coordinated. Most normal children show many of the signs mentioned; however, having them does not mean that the child is a musical genius, but only that the child is musical or receptive to music. A parent, seeing his child do these things,should take the responsibility of encouraging the child. Signs of musical genius or giftedness often do appear at an early age. These musical manifestations are so extraordinary that it is clear that the child is a musical prodigy. (More details are given in the chapter on the "Gifted Child").

One reason for providing music lessons to the child is that the parents have always wanted to be able to play a musical instrument and never had the opportunity. Now that they are parents, they believe that they should give that chance to their children. While this is a generous gesture for parents who grew up in homes with few opportunities and who worked hard to achieve a good standard of living which they can provide to their child now, it is important to remember to be generous, but not foolish. Too much of a good thing can be as harmful as too little! In wanting to do things for one's child, a parent should remember not to overwhelm the child with too many lessons. Lessons in tennis, riding, swimming,dancing and skating may be too much! It is important to make sure that a child has a well balanced life. A very important part of growing up is having the time and the opportunity to think, to play and to assimilate the abundance of information provided in the name of a "well-rounded" education. Many children are also subjected to academic pressure which means a lot of school work has to be done daily. If a parent adds private lessons in dance, tennis, etc. as well as music, to the academic pursuits, then the demand for the child's time becomes overwhelming. Music lessons will probably be the first to be given up.

It is important for the parents to make an assessment of the child's readiness for music. Some children are fascinated with exploring the piano and making up music and songs. Others may sing or listen to records. All of these children are showing by their interest that they could be receptive to music lessons. Before following up, it is important to think about the individual child; can he concentrate and follow through on a formal lesson? If the child is too young and seems very restless, then maybe the child belongs in some form of eurhythmics class where he can move and participate in other activities while learning about music. Or, if a class is not available, the musical parent can give small, five-minute lessons - teaching a small piece by rote or a little theory at different times throughout the day - until the child is ready for a full lesson.

Occasionally, a child who is still very young is ready for lessons and then it is important not to waste time in finding the right teacher. One musically precocious child of four whose parents finally found a piano teacher who would work with the child, was able to play the Bach D-minor piano concerto with the Boston Pops by the age of nine (the age at which many people think a child should just begin lessons). Most private teachers and institutions would not even discuss the request for lessons once they heard that he was only four years old. When the mother phoned, she was told, "He is too young to be taught." Because the mother was persistent, she finally found a teacher for the child. Studies of a number of musical prodigies reveal that most showed precocious musical ability and also started the study of an instrument at an early age.

Earlier we talked about signs of interest in music...singing along with music, "conducting", playing and repeating tunes on the piano, etc. Since the parent is in a unique position to know his own child very well, he must answer the question about how sustained the child's interest really is. Knowing your own child well is a big advantage. Some children show a few, well-developed interests and have long concentration spans at a very early age. If music happens to be an interest, then such a child would benefit by lessons. However, many young children flit from one activity to another. A hyperactive child who has no patience should start lessons at a later age. In one particular family, the eldest boy was hyperactive and unable to concentrate on music lessons until the age of nine. However, his younger brothers who had longer attention spans began music lessons at earlier ages. The youngest child at five showed a great interest in the piano, playing his older brother's piano music by ear. The middle child, at six, was able to concentrate on tasks for long periods of time and he, too, could start music lessons. Another sign of readiness for music lessons is patience - is the child willing to repeat tasks over and over until he gets them right as opposed to having a low frustration tolerance level and exploding at the first sign of failure? Since frustration tolerance level increases with age, children who are not ready for lessons at a young age may be ready at age of eight or nine years.

The parent should also take into consideration the child's eye-and-hand- coordination and motor coordination. "Does the child have difficulty in printing? in reading? What kind of games does he prefer - large motor (running, jumping) or reading, puzzles, drawing or other small motor activities? Does he like making tiny models or putting together intricate picture puzzles? What is his preference in art work... does he make detailed drawings or paint bold swathes of color? Does he make free form clay sculptures, or does he have the patience to form perfectly symmetrical pots? Does the child have learning disabilities? Does he see letters backwards or have difficulty grasping the whole sentence when he reads? How much strength does the child have - in his fingers, his wrists? How dexterous are his fingers? Are they long or short? Can he combine separate motions of both hands at the same time? - bowing with one and fingering with the other? (movements he will encounter in string playing.) What are the size of the child's hands and arm-span - can he reach what he needs to reach with ease? Is there a child-sized instrument that he might play? (Trombones come in one size only; violins come in several sizes.) Also, does he have mathematical aptitude? If he likes and understands mathematics, then the counting, and the rhythmical structure of music will be easier for him to understand.

The question of talent is always raised. Certain aspects of musical talent are helpful in learning music. If the child has a good sense of rhythm, good memory, a good ear (though not necessarily perfect pitch), understands explanations without too much repetition by the teacher, and is able to carry over what he learns to new tasks, music lessons will be more successful and will progress more rapidly.

One last thing to keep in mind for successful lessons is the suitability of the musical instrument to the particular child. Violinists depend more on their ears for finding the correct pitch or tone. Children with braces on their teeth have a harder time on a wind instrument, but the task is not impossible. A child whose small motor coordination is poor might have more trouble on the piano or clarinet (where he needs to be more precise with finger movements) than on trombone where he uses larger movements. However, a small child would have difficulty playing the trombone, if his arms were unable to reach the 7th position (fully extended). A tone-deaf trombonist would have difficulty, too, because the notes on trombone are judged by ear. If the child has one normal arm and one artificial limb, he might take up French horn; however, it is a difficult instrument to play and the parent would do well to consider the child's patience, interest and willingness to work long hours.

Interesting a child in music will be made a lot simpler if there is some interest or support from his peers or the local school system, or even from friends taking lessons, or other siblings in the family. What his friends are doing as well as their opinions make a great deal of difference to a child. If learning to play an instrument means the child can participate in the school band or other musical events, there will be an incentive to learn. Some schools provide an individualized credit system, which allows the child to spend his time on music while providing him with school credit and substituting music for other school subjects. If the school will not permit this, music lessons sometimes become a heavy time burden. If other friends or members of the same family are taking lessons, it makes it easier on the child.

One child who came from a neighborhood where taking music lessons was unusual finally quit,even though she was making excellent progress.Her mother was heartbroken, but the child simply couldn't stand up to the pressure of her friends, "Why do you take music lessons?"...Her peers made fun of her because they were jealous. If the teacher had known earlier what was happening, some positive steps could have been taken such as communicating with the principal of the school and some of the teachers, to let them know the child was special and the music teacher and the school could have worked together.

A Parent's Responsibilities in Regard to Music Lessons

Once the decision to take music lessons has been made, the parent has new responsibilities. One responsibility is financial. Music lessons are expensive - even for beginners; advanced lessons may place even more of a financial burden on the family. Parents may have to make special sacrifices to give the child lessons, foregoing a vacation trip, entertainment or a new piece of furniture. Another responsibility may be chauffering the child to lessons, recitals and concerts. If the child's teacher lives in the neighborhood or if the teacher comes to the home, there may not be such a time sacrifice. However, a child's musical education can be demanding. One parent who wanted special lessons only available in New York, spent weekends on the train with her two young children. Other families drive to New York from New Hampshire or Boston or Maine, etc. (a four to five hour trip one way, with extra expenses for meals, gas, etc.) so that their children may take advantage of the extensive musical education available at the Juilliard School.

A parent should also realize that if a child wants to achieve in music, he may not be able to achieve academically, too, because of lack of time. In a "tracked" school system he may have to settle for "honor" or "standard" courses rather than "advanced placement" courses. However, most children who do well in music are good students, too.

With respect to musical achievement, the parent should ask himself: am I pushing or supporting the child? There may be a fine dividing line. An extreme example is the child prodigy who was made to practice several hours a day and to give many recitals and appearances when very young. However, when the parent is so anxious for a child to succeed, the child's life can become miserable from practice and pressure. On the other hand, some parents slow down the child's gallop into musical achievement, wanting the children to have balance and diversity in education. It is not an easy road to take.

A wise parent who has thought through all her reasons and motives for wanting to give her child lessons, who has carefully considered whether her child is ready, and how the music lessons will be handled, will have an easier time of it and there will be a greater chance for success in the music lessons.

CHOOSING AN INSTRUMENT

Choosing the first instrument for a child to play is an important step for both the parent and the child. The age of the child makes a difference; if he is six years of age or younger, the choice of instruments that he will be capable of playing is very limited. The child can begin the piano...if he has the desire to learn the instrument, good motor coordination, and an adequate attention span. The child can begin lessons as early as three years old on a small violin or cello. (He will probably learn by the Suzuki method which does not require the ability to read music.) Another choice, if the child is able to handle it, is the recorder.

The most important factor in a young child's success is his desire and interest in learning to play the instrument. Before the age of six, the desire and impetus must come from the child, rather than from the adult. Most children are not ready to begin instrumental study before the age of six. However, as we mentioned earlier, they can benefit from a group musical experience.

Between the ages of six and eight years, the piano, recorder, violin, cello, percussion instruments and occasionally, the guitar, organ and harp, may be started. Most of the wind instruments should not be started before the age of nine or older because they require strength and breath control. Children can also learn to sing at an early age, but it is recommended that the singing be done in a group or chorus; it is advisable to wait until the child is at least 16 years old before starting vocal training so that the voice is not damaged.

Piano

The piano requires good hand and eye coordination and the ability to deal with at least two lines of melody or a line of melody in one hand and chords in the other. The process of reading and playing music is a complicated process. It involves seeing the printed page, understanding the meaning, then translating it through physically touching the piano and listening to what's played (feedback). The piano can be a satisfying instrument because it is a complete solo instrument. It can recreate any music in the Western repertoire and it is also the basis of harmony and counterpoint. The piano can be used to accompany voice and and the other instruments. It is used in orchestras occasionally, but is frequently used for combos and jazz bands. There is an almost limitless repertoire for the piano in early, contemporary,classical, pop and jazz music. Knowledge acquired in piano lessons is transferable to other instruments and is an aid in composing and arranging.

Recorder

The recorder is a relatively inexpensive instrument that can be studied by young children either in group instruction or in private lessons. Since there is no reed involved, it is a relatively simple instrument to learn. Although the recorder comes in different sizes and ranges such as F-sopranino, C-soprano, F-alto, C-tenor, and F-bass, each individual recorder is limited to a specific key. Techniques learned on the recorder can be transferred to other woodwind instruments. There is a body of recorder music written for solo as well as for an ensemble group of recorders (alto, tenor, etc.) There is also a lot of early chamber music literature available for the recorder.

Violin and Stringed Instruments

Another instrument which can be started as young as age three is the violin. However, it requires certain abilities if the child is to make progress. First of all, the child must have a discerning ear so that he can recognize whether he is producing the correct pitch and tone. Some of this can be learned, but the child needs some natural ability or he will feel frustrated and give up. Good coordination of arms, shoulders and fingers are needed as well as the ability to coordinate different types of movements. A child must have the stamina to maintain an awkward body position for many hours. The beginning sounds made on a violin are not especially pleasant for the listener, and the parents or family must be patient while the child learns. It takes much longer to produce a good,pleasing sound on the stringed instruments than it does on the other instruments. The child will need a lot of patience and perseverance if he is to succeed on a stringed instrument. An advantage of playing the stringed instruments is the abundance of literature: solo, instrumental, quartets, trios and chamber music as well as orchestral. With the exception of the cello and double bass, the stringed instruments are extremely portable. Because the stringed instruments are manufactured in less than full size, they can be started at an earlier age than the woodwinds. String learning is transferable ; a violinist can take up the viola without much difficulty and the cellist can play double bass.

Percussion Instruments

Percussion instruments and the drum,in particular, can be started at an early age, even before the age of nine. A fine and steady sense of rhythm and good coordination are important. Drummers and percussionists are in high demand for bands and orchestras, rock and jazz or popular music. Parents sometimes worry that they will not be able to stand the sound of practicing. They should realize that much of the beginning work can be done rather quietly on a practice pad. Other percussion instruments, such as the marimba, have a "sweeter" sound. However, the purchase of a complete percussion set is very costly.

Guitar

A stringed instrument that can be studied in several ways, depending on the child's interest and skills, is the guitar. Three basic kinds of guitars are available: the Western guitar, equipped with steel strings and played by a pick, a Spanish guitar strung with gut or nylon and plucked by the fingers, and the electric guitar which requires a source of power and amplification and is strung with steel.

There are also different styles of guitar music. The simplest is folk music (which can be played on either the Western guitar or the Spanish guitar). This makes a good "social" skill and is useful for accompanying a singer or a group.Emphasis is on the learning of chords. It helps if a child has a feeling for harmony so that he chooses the appropriate chords. Classical guitar literature is played on the Spanish guitar; there is a large body of literature with a lot of music transcribed from lute, harpsichord, clavier, etc. The Spanish guitar is often played as a solo instrument; the back-to-classical-guitar movement is a recent innovation started by Andrés Segovia. Flamenco is a style of playing which relies on a body of music that has been handed down from player to player without being written down. It requires a teacher, a good musical ear and memory, and the ability to improvise. Electric guitar is taught from music books. The emphasis is on learning a line of melody and/or the chords. Most music for electric guitar is in the rock or popular vein although there has been some experimentation with electric guitar by contemporary and classical composers, such as Daniel Pinkham. Electric guitar music may indicate only the chords by symbols; the player improvises on the bass chords provided.The electric guitar is in demand for rock bands and for popular music.

Harp

Children as young as eight years old can learn to play the harp if they are not too small. The harp is one of the most difficult instruments to learn, but beginners can play tunes after a few weeks. Parents may not be eager to start a child on harp because of the difficulty in transporting the instrument (it weighs 70 lbs.), the expense of buying it, and the nuisance of replacing broken strings frequently. A smaller harp, such as a newer, lightweight Troubadour, is much less expensive than the standard harp and also very easy to carry.

Wind Instruments

At the age of 9 or 10, many children want to begin the study of a brass or woodwind instrument - a flute, clarinet, saxophone, oboe, trumpet, trombone, French horn, tuba, etc. (Most elementary school bands start children at this age so that it becomes an "in" thing to do.) A lot of children begin instrumental study at this age in school, but a number of them drop out. It helps if the child likes the sound or chooses the instrument on his own.

For example, a child had studied violin in school and had hated the instrument. When the Band Director offered him the use of a trombone if he would take lessons, he jumped at the chance. However, it was not an easy instrument to play. Nevertheless, his interest and stubbornness(plus the support of his teacher and parents) prevailed while his trombone playing improved greatly. Another child balked at piano lessons but fell in love with the sound and look of the saxophone (the buttons and complicated structure fascinated him). Music lessons (which were becoming increasingly frustrating for him on the piano) now became a joy for him on the saxophone. His love for music eventually resulted in an interest in composing. This has since led back to a genuine interest in playing the piano now that he wants to hear how his own compositions

sound! It may be a difficult task for the parent, but
he should trust the child's inclination for a particular instrument if the child's interest seems genuine.

Flute and Piccolo

In wind instruments, the flute has certain advantages. There is no reed involved in playing and therefore no pressure on a mouthpiece; both factors are
helpful for a child who is having orthodontic treatment. The flute is small, lightweight, and doesn't
require much wind to play it; this makes it more suit-
able for a handicapped child, unless holding the arms
out to the side presents a problem. However,advanced
and professional playing requires good breath control.
Flute repertoire is extensive, starting with early music, ensembles, orchestra and band music. Knowledge
acquired in playing the flute is transferable to the
piccolo; fingering is nearly identical for the two instruments.

The other woodwind instruments...clarinets, saxophone, oboe and bassoon, all require the use of a reed
...a thin piece of wood that vibrates against the
mouthpiece to produce a tone. Reeds come in various
strengths; the child changes the strength of reed as
he progresses. Parents should realize that proper
mouthpieces and frequent reed changes are needed. A
child who must wear braces on his teeth will have some
difficulties in playing. The embouchure (position of
the mouth and lips) requires pulling in the lower jaw.
Playing woodwinds is helpful for the child who has an
underbite, but not too helpful if the child has protruding upper teeth. However, the length of time spent
in practice will probably not cause any real problems.
Metal braces may hurt the mouth, but the pain can be
avoided by wearing a rubber piece while practicing or
by placing wax over protruding parts of the braces.
The teeth may hurt after the braces have been tighten-
ed so the child may have to stop playing the instrument for a day or two until the mouth can stand the
pressure again.

31

Saxophone

Probably the easiest woodwind for a child to learn to play is the saxophone. Notes are produced by depressing buttons. The sound is pleasing so that a beginning saxophone player does not have to wait long to achieve a good sound. Of course, the silken tone and vibrato of professional artists take many years to perfect. The main problem in playing the saxophone is that it is a relative latecomer in the development of instruments so that the musical literature is somewhat scarce. In the case of a child who prefers to play classical saxophone music, it is usually very difficult to play and is written in contemporary style. The saxophone is in great demand for symphonic bands, but much less for orchestras. The saxophone is a staple for jazz bands and for bands playing popular music. Most children start saxophone lessons on the alto. Learning can then be transferred to tenor, baritone and soprano saxophone. However, the latter instruments require more wind, plus a slightly different embouchure and playing technique (which can be greatly helped through lessons). If a child is serious about becoming a musician, and is anxious to have more opportunities to play in orchestras and bands, but has started on the saxophone, he may want to consider learning clarinet. One of the registers on the clarinet is identical to that of the saxophone, so that the saxophone playing is partially transferable. However, the easier transition is made from the clarinet to saxophone.

Clarinet

The clarinet also requires a mouthpiece and reed, but more wind and skill to play it than the saxophone. It requires the learning of a second register and is played by covering up holes on the body of the instrument rather than by depressing buttons. This takes finer coordination and can be frustrating for a young child. Compared to what is available for the saxophone, clarinet literature is extensive. (However, the modern clarinet dates back only to 1800.) Music for clarinet is available from the time of Mozart (1760 - 1780) - concertos, woodwind chamber music, solo instrumental music, etc. The clarinet has even found a place in jazz; for example, Dixieland and Benny Goodman's big band music. Generally, it is not used in the "big band" sound which usually has trombones,saxophones and trumpets. A clarinet player can easily transfer from playing the usual Bb clarinet to an "A" or "Eb" clarinet and the bass clarinet, all of which are used in orchestral music.

Oboe and Bassoon

Learning to play the oboe is a much more difficult task. Because no mouthpiece is used, the player makes the sound by blowing on and vibrating a double set of reeds. This gives beginning players much more difficulty. More advanced players must learn to make their own reeds. Learning to play oboe demands great perseverance; however, good oboists are in big demand for bands, orchestras, and chamber music.Oboe players can also learn to play bassoon, another instrument which is also used a lot in orchestras, bands and some ensemble music, for many of the same reasons as the oboe. Another double-reed instrument, which oboists can play, is the English horn, mostly used in orchestral music.

The remaining set of wind instruments,the brasses, is in great demand for bands, orchestras and jazz groups. There is a lot of music written for brass instruments: early music literature, orchestral and popular music.

Trumpet

The trumpet is probably the most popular brass instrument. It is played with a mouthpiece and without a reed. Notes are formed by depressing the valves while the mouth forms various positions. If the child wears braces, playing can be difficult, but wax or a rubber insert for the mouth can be used. If there are problems,these can be checked out with the orthodontist.

Trombone

Trombone playing is similar to trumpet playing. A mouthpiece is used but instead of using valves to produce notes, the player changes the position of the slide with his hand. The trombone player depends on his hearing and musical memory to play the correct note. Pitch and tone tend to improve with practice. A certain amount of strength, stamina and perseverance are needed to succeed at trombone playing; also, there is very little solo repertoire available for trombone.

Baritone Horn and Tuba

Another brass instrument, the baritone horn, plays the same range as the trombone, but it is easier to play since the baritone horn produces notes through the use of valves, rather than a slide. The tuba is similar to the baritone horn, but larger. Both instruments are used in symphonic and marching bands and orchestras. There isn't much solo repertoire for either baritone horn or tuba with the exception of some contemporary music.

French Horn

The French horn is an instrument with a unique and beautiful sound, but it is very difficult to play. Skilled French horn players are much sought after, but the task of learning to play well is arduous. Although the horn has a great range, most beginners concentrate on one end of the range because it is easier. There is a large French horn repertoire, mainly orchestral and chamber music with some solo literature.

A SURVEY OF AVAILABLE MUSIC LESSONS AND EDUCATION

In one city, a child of nine commemorates his fifth year of piano lessons by playing a concerto with a symphony orchestra while another 9 year old has his first piano lesson. A group of preschoolers gives an impressive violin concert while an older violinist performs as a soloist with a youth symphony. On the football field, the bands of two opposing high school teams march and play a piece to cheer their teams on; later that night a musical is presented with student soloists.

All of these children have had some musical instruction and most of it was probably arranged and paid for by their parents. The kinds of music instruction each has had varies. Certain types of instruction may not be available everywhere throughout the country. However, a brief survey of the various kinds of music lessons which may be available should make the parent's choice a bit easier.

Music Education in School

It should be pointed out that even if the parent does not make an effort to find music lessons for the child, most children will receive their first organized introduction to music in school by singing, listening to records, or through simple lessons in reading music. Many school systems also have programs for children who express a particular interest or talent in music. (The talent might be judged by a music supervisor or teacher who uses either an established music test or a test devised by the school.) Music participation might involve school bands, choruses, orchestras, etc. In some schools, beginning instrumental lessons on strings, brasses, woodwinds, and percussion instruments are provided by the school during the regular classroom time.

Church Music

Children may also be exposed to music in churches or synagogues. During services children may sing along with the congregation or they may hear trained musicians and the powerful strains of the organ. This provides a wonderful opportunity to experience "live"music and may be a child's first such experience. Some churches organize boys' or children's choirs which might require an audition before the child is accepted for membership. The choirs hold rehearsals and training as well as a weekly performance during church services.

Other musical training, in addition to what we have just mentioned, will have to be arranged and paid for by the parents. Since there are many different kinds of lessons and music schools available, we will explain some of the advantages and some of the disadvantages of each arrangement to help parents make a more intelligent choice for the child.

The Neighborhood Music Teacher

Probably the most familiar music teacher is the one who teaches in the neighborhood. This teacher has often had a controversial reputation despite the fact that he or she has carried out one of the most important tasks in the history of American music. Although everyone knows a story or two to tell about the problems of lessons with a neighborhood music teacher,more often than not,this individual has been a real pillar of the community and town.

Of course, there are some problems connected with the neighborhood music teacher. Some teachers have a poor background in music, thereby providing few pedagogical resources, and limited intellectual and technical stimulation.Unlike England,Canada or other countries previously affiliated with the British Kingdom, where each teacher must be certified by the Royal Conservatory of Music before he or she can get a license to teach,anyone can set up shop and teach in the United States. In a small town with a population of 2000 people, there may be only one teacher available, so there would be no choice at all. A teacher from a very small town, even if properly trained, has problems of: isolation from musical colleagues, the lack of opportunity of being connected with a teaching institution, the "cross-pollination" of ideas a teacher can get from hearing students of other teachers, a dearth of exposure to new music, and a lack of opportunity to discuss ideas with other teachers. Isolation generally causes all the problems associated with the neighborhood music teacher. It is the main reason for any lack of motivation in such a teacher.

On the other hand, many neighborhood music teachers are graduates of music schools with diplomas, degrees and impeccable credentials. These teachers have the advantage of offering lessons in the neighborhood at either the teacher's or the student's home. Lesson fees are usually cheaper because the teacher does not have to split the fee with an institution. An interested and devoted teacher will also arrange workshops so that the students can hear each other and he will also have recitals at least once a year. If the teacher is active in musical associations, he can help arrange for the child to go to auditions and competitions. The teacher may promote concert-going by encouraging or telling the children what is available, sometimes even arranging excursions. Another service that the neighborhood teacher performs is to provide music books for the student for which the student then reimburses the teacher. This saves on extra trips to the music store and cuts down on delays in purchasing a book.

There are many advantages to using the neighborhood music teacher; however, the parent must take the responsibility of doing some research and finding out about the teacher before the child signs up for lessons.

In the greater Boston area, there is a large number of excellent private teachers who are organized under the auspices of the New England Piano Teachers Association and the Massachusetts Music Teachers Association. These organizations serve the teachers, students and the community admirably by providing workshops, seminars, recitals and competitions. This effectively removes the "isolation barrier"that private teachers have to overcome.

Music Schools Sponsored by Public Schools

Another source for music lessons is a Music School under the auspices of the public school. This is a very convenient arrangement which should work well. The main advantage of this arrangement is that the student receives a lesson at school and does not have to travel. Rates are usually cheaper, which is helpful to the parents; unfortunately, the faculty usually is paid very little. This leads to a transient faculty, or a situation where the teachers may be of poor quality or lack in teaching experience. Lessons may be held in several different school buildings located around the town. There may be little communication between teachers and the Director and very little supervision of teachers. Pianos and studios may also vary in quality. Of course, the exception to this situation occurs when there is an outstanding music supervisor in the school system and the school department is willing to subsidize the music school. Before the parent enrolls the child for lessons, he should investigate the school carefully.

Group Lessons

Group lessons, which often take place in school or at a music school connected with a public school, are a wonderful way of starting a child in music because of the social aspect of learning with other children who are working on a common activity. The positive aspects of group lessons are: the sharing of lessons with peers, the stimulation of hearing others and a development of "healthy" competition, the indirect repetition and solidifying of basics through hearing others, and the friendship and communication the child receives from other music makers.

On the negative side, group lessons fail when the group is so large that a slow or advanced child has to be neglected for the purpose of keeping a certain pace. We do not recommend more than two years of group lessons unless the child has some private lessons also. In some schools where group instrumental lessons are provided, one teacher may teach several instruments - trumpet, saxophone, trombone, percussion,clarinet,etc. This may be economical,but it is not the best arrangement for learning proper technique because the teacher may lack the experience or knowledge required to teach all instruments perfectly.

The Community Music School

Another place that offers music lessons is the Community Music School or Community Arts Center. This neighborhood center, devoted to the arts for everyone, is conveniently located and tries to be responsive to the needs of the community. Community Music Schools vary depending on where the School is located (urban vs.rural setting,poor vs.rich community) and how much financial backing it has.

How does a parent assess or judge a Community Music School? One way is to ask whether the School belongs to the Guild of Community Music Schools. If it does, it must meet certain standards of structure,curriculum, and professional staffing.The parent can rest assured that the School will have high standards. Not every good school chooses to belong. However,the parent should seek information about the School's reputation, have a personal interview with the Director, and make careful studies of brochures to find out about courses offered, the teachers and their qualifications.

Unfortunately, one of the biggest problems that some Community Music Schools face is the everlasting quest for financial support so that they can offer programs at reasonable rates.Financially strapped schools often have faculty who are poorly paid, or are poorly trained or transient. Music education may be uneven in quality.

The Community Music School can offer a lot.In addition to providing concerts, workshops, theory programs, ensembles, orchestras and choruses, it has the advantage of offering grass-roots programs, of trying out new ideas for interaction among the various art disciplines, and of providing adult programs and community services. At times, the Community Music School fulfills the role of the mini-conservatory when there are no Universities or Conservatories located nearby.

Preparatory or Extension Departments

Another source of music lessons is the Preparatory or Extension Department of a Conservatory or University. Preparatory Departments have certain inherent problems. Because they are the stepchildren of the mother institution, they may charge a high fee. In addition to the Conservatory or University faculty,the staff may include student teachers or retiring faculty who are being pushed out of the institution. There is often confusion or a lack of philosophical goals.Sometimes the schools are used to make money for the mother institution. As far back as 1926, Alexander Siloti, the Russian musician and pianist, pointed out that the European system through government subsidy made it possible to maintain high artistic ideals because the schools did not have to be run for profit with the money made from the teacher's work and student's tuition.

On the other hand, the Preparatory School can be very good. Because it has the use of the facilities from the larger institution, it may have better practice halls and instruments, a library, a record collection, good concert halls, perhaps even a music store. Some of the schools run graded or Certificate programs with a well-rounded program of private les-

40

sons, theory, ensembles, workshops and recitals.(Children follow a prescribed program of study at different levels such as: beginner, junior,intermediate and senior.) A child taking lessons at a Preparatory School will meet other children who are deeply involved in music and he will feel a sense of community with musicians, something which most other music lessons lack. Many Preparatory Schools do an excellent job of pre-professional training.

We have outlined many possibilities for music lessons: the neighborhood music teacher, the music school lessons, group lessons, the Community Music school and the Preparatory Department of a Conservatory or a University. It is important to carefully analyze each child's talents and interests. It is not too difficult to change institutions as the child grows musically ambitious (or less ambitious) as long as healthy and intelligent communication exists among the child, parent and the teacher. Since each child is different and there are many choices in music, the proper choice can bring much happiness and development in the life of the individual. In the quest for the right choice at any one particular moment, we believe that there are no substitutes for professionalism and high standards, no matter what the level of musicianship.

THE IDEAL TEACHER

A good music teacher is born with a special feeling for teaching, a love of music, an ability to relate to and communicate with children, a flexibility and receptivity to new ideas and new ways of teaching. Even if a teacher has many degrees and diplomas hanging on the wall and is an outstanding performer,he may still be a poor teacher. Though music education may enhance and refine and develop his teaching technique, the basic qualities that go to make up a good teacher are inborn.

One will not find a good teacher "play acting" or putting on a "mask" when he talks to a child. Instead he will relate directly to the child. He will avoid gimmicks or getting "into character". Children do have an uncanny knack of seeing right through poses and impostors. A teacher should be straight-forward and sincere, energetic, imaginative - a creative Pied Piper. It is of paramount importance that the teacher be teaching as a matter of choice, not because he is embittered because he never performed in Carnegie Hall. One who mourns for a lost career passes on the bitterness and frustrations to his pupils.

The Student Is an Individual

Parents want the teacher to see each child as an individual, not just as a pupil to whom a carbon copy lesson plan can be assigned. In the same way that no two children are alike, no two lessons plans can be alike; teaching should and must be done on an individual basis. A good teacher is, in a way, a good doctor who prescribes a course of treatment. He must be willing to put forth the effort needed to find out something about a child and his particular needs and then make an effort to find a way to teach the pupil so that the child has joy in the music and develops his full musical potential. For example, a teacher who has a pupil whose sibling is a talented and outstanding young musician, must find different music for his pupil, so that there is no invidious comparison with the sibling. Also, the child can be encouraged to learn another instrument on which he may prove to be as gifted as his sibling.

Prescribing what's good for the individual child requires a certain flexibility on the part of the teacher. One teacher whose gifted pupil was planning to play a concerto in a competition was chagrined to learn that the girl had broken her wrist. The teacher wisely controlled her anguish, gave the pupil a pep talk and told her to pick up the Scriabin Nocturne for the Left Hand on her way home from the hospital. The girl learned the piece and was able to perform it three weeks later. Her success led to the realization that she had power in her left hand; subsequently she learned the Ravel Concerto for the Left Hand. What had been a crisis was turned into a learning opportunity by a flexible and wise teacher.

The good teacher has to adjust his teaching to each individual child. There are a number of common situations that the teacher may meet and the ideal teacher will find good solutions for them.

Some students may come from another teacher. If a student is talented, the previous teacher may have been anxious to exploit that talent and may have skipped the basics of technique, letting the child go ahead to big and flashy pieces. (One young child was already playing the music of Brahms before he had studied any music of Bach.) The task of the new teacher is clear: to fill in the missing technique. The good teacher will have to take the student back to the basics, teaching Bach, simpler Mozart pieces and working with technique (scales and exercises).

Another problem is how to deal with a child whose parents believe that the child is "another Mozart". The good teacher must help the parents put the child's talent into perspective. The teacher can have the parents listen to other gifted students.

Some students may have had teachers who did not recognize their talent or did nothing to develop it. The good teacher will assign extra music, provide a longer lesson time, encourage more performances, the playing in ensemble groups, taking theory classes, etc. The new teacher has an important role to play in the process of bringing out the hidden or undeveloped talent of the student.

Some children have had bad experiences with their previous teachers. The children may have been rushed or pushed into performing before they felt that they were ready for it. At the other extreme, they may have been held back from learning as much as they could. Or, they may have had a teacher who squelched all joy in learning by his way of teaching. Some children may need their confidence bolstered.

An important role played by the teacher is to be a good friend to a child and, in a way, almost a member of the child's family. To be an effective teacher, he or she must keep all the avenues of communication open, yet remember that the purpose of the weekly meeting is the lesson rather than just friendship. The teacher must keep some perspective about the relationship, controlling the lesson and controlling the friendship. Although it is not necessary to turn the music studio into a psychiatrist's office, it is hard to imagine a teacher who could be effective without understanding the whole child. The bond formed between teacher and the student can be of enormous help (both in learning music and in the development of the child's personality).

Because most actual teaching of music is done on a one-to-one basis, a particularly interested and caring teacher can exert a very strong and positive influence on the child. The development of friendship and mutual trust with an adult outside the family can often be the basis for surviving the temptations and difficulties of the teenaged years. A teacher may find that the pupils' parents are calling on him or her to talk about problems with the children that the parents have been unable to discuss. The teacher may have such a good relationship with the child that the parents feel he is "the only adult to whom the child will talk or listen". In this world of increasing depersonalization, with learning done via teaching machines, large classes, and visual aids such as television, a music teacher working with a student in a one-to-one relationship provides a very valuable, very positive, and very rare teaching and learning situation.

The Teacher as a Resource Center

In addition to this special relationship between teacher and pupil, the teacher should be a resource center for musical activities. He must create an atmosphere of musical activity in his studio. Effort and planning must go into providing enrichment, expanding and exploring other facets of music such as symphonic repertoire, opera, songs and other instrumental music, carrying out workshops, recitals, and preparation for competitions. In addition, he should do a study of related materials such as history, architecture, poetry and politics which enhance the interpretation of a given piece of repertoire. This makes the study of music much more interesting. For example, the performance of a piece of music becomes more significant if the performer places the music in a historical context. For example, the minuet was danced in a salon, with all its formalities, in elaborate costumes and wigs. The music accompanied the dance with its curtsies and bows. This knowledge can be useful for the performer when he makes his interpretation of the music.

The teacher should be able to plan and carry out a workshop in such a way that it helps the children both musically and socially. Although a child might

45

be apprehensive at first, the teacher must handle the workshop so that the child will be eager to perform again. Whatever the child's presentation, even if it is only a scale, it should be treated with great importance and artistic care. A properly handled workshop will convey the feeling that everyone present is learning and contributing something; each can learn from the other's experiences and each can understand the other's performance at any given level of proficiency. Workshops and recitals help to create a feeling of community among the students. Learning to play an instrument is a lonely task so that there is something encouraging about attending a workshop where one child struggles with a piece of music that another has already mastered. A child can measure the distance he has traveled by listening to another child who is performing a piece that he already knows.

The good teacher must want to expand his musical horizons and to try new things. If he belongs to a music organization, he will attend lectures or classes, continuing to learn by being exposed to new ideas and new music. His learning should not stop when he finishes his degree. A good teacher should never stop playing and practicing for the practical reason of keeping abreast of his own students. It will help his teaching and improve his explanations, and expand and secure his own knowledge.

A teacher who was planning an all-Stravinsky concert for his students decided to do some research for it. He found an old newspaper clipping from the Paris Le Figaro. It had a small waltz which Stravinsky had written as a souvenir for the interviewer (the waltz had never been published.) The piece was included in the program, becoming the talk of the day. The student who was chosen to play it was very proud of giving that waltz its first Boston performance. Of course, this took an expenditure of effort by the teacher far beyond that normally allotted for a lesson or a concert.

46

Similarly, a good teacher will read music journals and magazines, be aware of new discoveries and editions, the latest in musicology. He will browse in music stores for new and exciting music appropriate for each of his pupils. Proper preparation for teaching takes more effort than simply coming to the lesson and working with the child during the lesson.

A good teacher will be receptive to new ideas. A teacher who had taught Debussy's Children's Corner Suite for many years cringed when he first heard that someone had recorded an electronic music version.When the pupil brought in the record, the teacher discovered to his surprise that the music was delightful,that the arrangement by Isao Tomita is a subtle interpretation which brings out Debussy's ideas even better than they are expressed via the piano."Golliwog's Cakewalk", for example, originally written as a satire with barbs aimed at Wagner becomes even more humorous when the music is translated into "blip, blop, de blip" and bubling sounds of the electronic Moog synthesizer.

A teacher who loves the classics but who is faced with a child who loves popular music, may have to find a way of introducing classical music subtly to the child. David Brubeck's Themes from Eurasia contains several simple jazz arrangements using classical foundations (Brubeck studied with Darius Milhaud).A child who can play more difficult arrangements might be eased into the classics via Scott Joplin's Rags or contemporary music such as Roy Harris's arrangement of"Black is the Color of My True Love's Hair".

A teacher should be flexible. A clarinet teacher had a pupil who knew a lot of music theory, but had limited technique. He gave the child a variety of music to hold his interest. However, he assigned sections of the advanced pieces that he was certain the child could master. This gave the child some variety of music, yet didn't penalize or frustrate him for playing an instrument (clarinet) that has very little repertoire or interesting beginning literature. The piano teacher does not have this problem because there is a lot of good beginning music.

Communication with Parents

A teacher who is willing to communicate with parents is preferable to a teacher who doesn't bother to establish a relationship. If a problem does arise,the teacher who has set up a relationship will be able to talk with the parents easily. Sometimes children do not show up for lessons (and the parent knows nothing about it if the teacher doesn't bother to tell him.) Perhaps, the child is unprepared for the lessons (sometimes with good reason), or there may be something happening at home that prevents the child from making good progress in the lessons, but the teacher has no way of finding this out unless he has an avenue of communication with the parents. A good teacher establishes the lines of communication from the beginning lessons.

Good teachers earn the respect of the parents. Some parents have notions of their own about how music should be taught. These ideas may conflict or contradict the teacher's ideas. Ideally, the teacher will be able to find a way of teaching the child that will ultimately win over the parents to the teacher's point of view. Occasionally, there may be parents with very strong ideas, and winning them over may be impossible. On the other hand, some parents have some good ideas, helpful knowledge, and understanding about the child which they should communicate to the teacher.

Occasionally the "chemistry" between the teacher and child is wrong. No matter how hard the teacher tries, it is impossible to feel right about a particular child. Reasons for this might include: the child may subconsciously remind the teacher of a disliked acquaintance or relative or perhaps the child has habits which irritate the teacher. One teacher may find it impossible to work with learning-disabled or slow children, while another may feel threatened whenever he has to work with gifted children. The point is that whatever the problem, the teacher should be sensitive enough to accept the fact that if something is wrong which can't be improved, a change of teacher should be gracefully accomplished. As long as an uncomfortable situation exists, the child won't learn much. On the other hand, sometimes the parents err in wanting to switch the child who is doing well and progressing nicely with a particular teacher because they have learned about another teacher who is more prestigious. This is the wrong reason for switching.   There may come a time when the child "outgrows" what the teacher has to offer and that is the right time to switch teachers.

Learning from Pupils

An experienced teacher should have an extensive knowledge of repertoire at all levels. There are certain pieces, etudes and exercises which are staples in the development of young performers, but it would be very monotonous for the teacher and his students if every step were prescribed. By working with his or her students, the teacher learns more about teaching from his students than he can from any class or book. One of the authors discovered a lot of information about trills and performance practices when he assigned a piece by Rameau to a pupil and then both exchanged library research on the period with each other.   From another student he learned about jazz rhythms when he assigned contemporary jazz pieces. One of his pupils playing a Chopin Etude approached it with a natural stroke that made the piece easier to play.   Another child played a very contemporary piece that the author had played many years earlier and picked up a few sharps that the author had missed in the playing.

The author who is a musician was asked to speak to a group of piano teachers on the subject of teaching teenagers. When he failed to come up with any original ideas for this musically sophisticated group of teachers, he asked his teenaged students to tell

49

him what it was he did to help them. One particularly bright and articulate boy put it this way - the three qualities he looked for in a good teacher were:

> guidance
> encouragement
> mutual trust and respect

The words of this teenager sum up the attributes of an ideal teacher better than we can!

BUYING AN INSTRUMENT

After the child has decided which instrument he wants to play, the next step is acquiring an instrument. Since the parent and teacher have no way of knowing with certainty if the child will stay with the instrument, it may be better to rent an instrument for beginning lessons.

There are several alternative arrangements that can be made. If the child begins his lessons in a school band, the school may have a supply of instruments to lend the child. He can try one out so that he is certain that he will stay with it before purchasing one. Some schools make arrangements with a music shop so that children can rent instruments for three months or for a trial rental period at a nominal cost.

Before renting the instrument, the parents should find out if it is possible to apply the rental price to the purchase of the instrument should the child decide to stay with it. In the case of stringed instruments, if there is no possibility of renting, the parents should find out whether the music shop will sell the instrument with the understanding that it can be traded in on a larger size when the child outgrows it. When pianos are rented, there is a large fee involved in the delivery and pick-up (which sometimes makes rental prohibitive). However, the parent might consider renting with the option to buy, applying the rental money toward the purchase.

On the other hand, if the instrument will be purchased eventually, it might be better to rent a new instrument rather than one which has been used by other children. This raises the question, is it better to buy a new or used instrument? In general, if the used instrument is a good brand (preferably a professional

51

model rather than a student model), it may be better to buy the older instrument rather than the cheaper, but newer, student model. A professional repairman or the teacher can be helpful in deciding the value or worth of a particular instrument. Ask around among music teachers and friends for a reputable place to buy the instrument. It may be helpful if the dealer has a repair service at the shop because instruments do get a lot of wear and tear and do need some minor repairs, and occasionally major ones. (Pads fall off, screws disappear and occasionally the instrument gets broken when a child trips over it!)

We mentioned the importance of having professional help in picking out an instrument. The music teacher (or in the case of the piano, a tuner) can evaluate the instrument for a moderate fee before the decision to buy is made. Keep in mind that new instruments, even of the same make and brand, will have individual variations, a slightly different sound and feel. They should be tried out in the shop so that the best available instrument is chosen. Even if the instrument chosen basically is a sound one, there may be minor adjustments needed. With the help of professional advice, problems can be identified and an agreement reached so that the adjustments are made, free of charge, before the instrument is purchased.

Since both student and professional models of most instruments are available, how does one decide what to buy? The decision should be made considering the cost, availability, and condition of the particular instrument. The instrument should be in good working condition or the child may feel so frustrated that he will not continue the lessons. In the case of the clarinet, it may be better for the child to start with a plastic model which does not require as careful cleaning as a wooden one. If not kept dry, a wooden clarinet may crack. Also, wood cracks from extremes of heat or cold. (Instruments should not be left in closed cars or near radiators, open windows, or in damp places.) Of course, the plastic may break if it is

52

dropped, but only a section of the clarinet will have to be replaced. There comes a time, however, when the teacher will suggest that the child needs a better instrument to continue making good progress. In the case of a stringed instrument, the child may simply need a bigger size because he has grown. On the other hand, if the child is serious about music, the parent may need to invest in a better and more expensive instrument. Although the same holds true for brass and woodwind instruments, the sound of these instruments can be improved by buying a new and better mouthpiece. In the case of woodwind instruments, a different strength, or a better reed, will improve the sound. For stringed instruments, a new bow might help improve the quality of the sound.

When renting or buying an instrument, it makes sense to take out some insurance (usually a floater policy can be added to the household insurance for very little money). If the instrument is either lost or stolen, the insurance will cover replacement.

Piano

If the child decides that he wants to take piano lessons, the parent is faced with a major purchase. Since a piano is a costly purchase, it should be considered in the same way as buying a car. (The piano will surely last a lot longer than the car!) Reputation, durability, quality, financing, depreciation, and need are important qualities to consider. In addition, the piano will serve an artistic, sensory, aesthetic and emotional function. If well cared for, the piano can last for 50 years and in some cases, even longer. Since the market for pianos is large and competitive, it is worth spending time in research before a purchase is made.

There is a large selection of different brands of pianos so that it pays to be careful in making a choice. Unfortunately, the piano is such a big piece of furniture that people sometimes tend to consider looks more important than function. A piano should be purchased for its practical use, not for how well it matches the furniture. However, for those who can afford it, pianos are made in many styles - early American, Italian Provincial, Contemporary, French Provincial, Traditional Mediterranean. The most elegant and classic piano is probably the traditional grand in ebony.

Even though a child is just a beginner, it should be realized that the artist and the amateur both need an excellent piano. It is a fallacy to think that the beginner should "make do" with any keyboard as long as it moves up and down. The professional or advanced student's demands from an instrument are not that different from the demands that should be made by a young student. The early years of training are really crucial in terms of developing and learning the techniques and art of playing the piano. Since these are the years in which to learn how to develop the gradations of touch and turn a beautiful phrase, a good piano is as essential to the beginner as to the professional.

The first step in buying a piano is to telephone the stores to find out the prices on both uprights or grands. Ask for brochures describing the pianos they carry. These brochures can be very informative when you compare several brands of pianos and learn about the differences among them. In addition,ask opinions from other piano owners, music teachers, piano tuners and professional performers. They will help evaluate the list and eliminate some brands from it.

Unfortunately, most piano teachers do not know much about the inside of the piano or about piano technology. However, the teacher can be helpful in making a decision because of knowledge of the reputation of certain pianos,and the teacher can certainly judge the tone quality and action of a particular piano.

A piano currently costs about $2,000 to $4,000

for a new upright or studio piano and some grand pianos start at $5,000 (for a 5-foot piano) and more,
depending on size. Before buying a piano, it would
be worthwhile to hire a piano technician for $20-$25
to help make the decision. He knows all about the
technical side of the piano, the scale design, the
strings, the tuning pins, the soundboard, the plates,
bridges, pin plank, hammers and dampers. In addition,
he will be able to tell a lot about the piano from the
serial number. Every piano has a number. By checking
in his book, he can tell in which year the piano was
made. This is important because some factories have
closed or have been bought out by other piano companies,
and it is important to know the history of the piano
you are buying-whether the craftsmanship was good, if
substitute materials were used, etc.

In considering a foreign piano, keep in mind that
European-made pianos cannot stand the dryness caused by
heating in this country. Use of a humidifier can help
both European and American manufactured pianos. If the
piano is to be used in a very hot and damp climate ,
then it needs to be treated by a process called
"tropicalization" (a process in which wood and strings
and other metal parts of the piano are coated so that
it can stand the heat and extreme humidity of tropical
climates). When one of the authors lived near the o-
cean, even tropicalization was not enough protection
for the piano. Twine was strung on the top of the piano
string frame and an Army blanket was draped over the
twine so as not to interfere with the mechanism of the
piano. This acted as a filter and kept the strings
from rusting.

In buying a used piano, follow most of the steps
outlined earlier. The only problem encountered will
be that a lot of old piano brands are no longer manufactured so that information on them is no longer a-
vailable. In this case, the advice of a piano technician is very important.

It is also a good idea to look at the classified

ads when buying a used piano. Stories of the couple leaving the country who cannot take along their piano and are selling their piano cheaply because they cannot wait, are true. We have seen this happen many times. With the help of a technician, it is possible to get a wonderful buy this way.

Suggestions on caring for a piano are: place it away from extremes of heat and cold, avoid spilling liquids in it and do not allow small children to play with the inside mechanism or to touch the strings.The outside of the piano can be cleaned with a slightly damp cloth, followed by a buffing with a dry cloth. Mild soap and water, followed by a rinse with a clean damp cloth, can be used if the piano is very dirty.Do not use commercial polishes on the cabinet of the piano. The piano should be tuned at least twice a year ...six weeks after dramatic changes of summer and winter weather.

Brass Instruments

When buying a brass instrument, it is wise to have the help of the teacher in choosing a particular model. If there is a choice between a good, used professional model of the instrument rather than a student model, the older one may be a better buy. If there are dents in the instrument, they may or may not be a problem, depending on where they are located. A dented or bent slide in a trombone is a major problem, but a dent in the bell part of the instrument only damages the looks, not the sound. In addition to the instrument, a mouthpiece will be needed.The teacher should advise the student on buying the mouthpiece as well as the instrument.

Brass instruments should be thoroughly cleaned in a tub about once each year with warm water and soap. Valves in trumpets, baritone horns or tubas are removed and washed. Valves need daily oiling to prevent sticking. Trombone slides should also be frequently cleaned and oiled to prevent sticking.

It is important to protect brass and other types of instruments with a sturdy case to prevent dents and other damage. Although there are lightweight cloth cases made for trumpets and some of the bigger instruments, these are not particularly protective or safe.

Woodwind Instruments

Buying a woodwind instrument also requires professional advice to help choose the best-sounding instrument. Beware of cracks in the wood of a clarinet. (Small cracks may be repaired, but large ones are a sign of trouble.) Remember that in addition to the particular instrument some difference in the sound is attributable to the choice of mouthpiece. Also, the strength of the reed affects the sound produced. As a student improves in his playing, he may need to buy sturdier reeds.

Buying and caring for a saxophone requires a process similar to that of the clarinet, although the saxophone is somewhat sturdier. Both clarinet and saxophone will need some repairing to replace worn or missing pads. The joints on the clarinet and the place where the mouthpiece joins the body of the instrument need to be lubricated with cork grease.

The oboe is an instrument similar in construction to the clarinet. Student models are made in plastic and professional ones are made of wood. The biggest problem for beginning oboist is to learn how to make his own reeds. Plastic reeds and ready-made cane reeds can be purchased, but they do not produce a very good tone. Bassoons are similar to oboes with respect to the reeds, but are much more expensive to purchase (a professional bassoon can cost $2,500) so we recommend expert advice for purchase.

Stringed Instruments

Buying of string instruments requires finding the correct size to buy for the particular child. Instruments are made in ½ to full size and violins are made in 1/4, 1/8 and 1/16 size. Correct size for a violin is judged by the position of the elbow (making a V of the left arm when in a playing position.) For a cello, the child should be able to reach all the strings easily with the tip of the bow. A major third should be easily reached with the right hand as well as a whole step between the second and first fingers. For a string bass, the right hand must be able to place the tip of the bow on all four strings without straining. The left hand has to reach a major second from first to fourth fingers.

For the stringed instruments, bows are important pieces of equipment. They should be the proper size for the instrument. Pegs for tuning should be easy to turn (the adult will have to do the tuning if the child is not strong enough).

There are many grades of quality in stringed instruments. Cheaper ones may be serviceable, but will not produce the finer and mellower tone required by an artist. As the child increases his level of playing, he will want a better model. Some of the finest stringed instruments are extremely old and very valuable, very expensive to purchase and difficult to acquire.

Caring for the stringed instruments consists of preventive medicine...putting the instrument away carefully so that it doesn't break.The student should also learn how to clean the instrument, how to tune the strings (when he's older) and how to replace them. He should know how to adjust and line up the bridge and how to tighten and loosen the bow to correct tautness and slackness.

The value of a guitar increases with age, but a guitar of poor quality will deteriorate by warping and cracking or the wooden parts may separate. Cheap guitars which have been imported from warm climates often crack when brought into a cold climate. One does not have to spend a fortune buying a guitar, but a moderate amount will purchase an instrument of good quality. A guitar does not require much care except protection from accidental bumps. It is helpful to learn how to tune it and how to replace broken strings without help.

* * * * * * * * *

Instruments are the media with which we make our music. Their value is not measured solely in a materialistic way. Respect and good habits in the care of the instrument are qualities which should be instilled in the student from the very beginning.

BEGINNING LESSONS

First lessons should convey the joy and excitement of learning to play the instrument, producing a
satisfying sound, and beginning to read music. For
very young children the instrument and rudiments of
music may be explored by rote with the use of a book
for a few weeks.

The First Music Book

Children experience great joy when they get their
first music book.The book is tangible and is physical
proof of the music lessons, something the child can
take home with him. The special meaning of the book
to the child is apparent at once. Children arrive at
a music lesson with a new book and often open it to a
favorite title. They might ask the teacher to play
the last page (because they think it is the most difficult piece). They show great awe and excitement
when hearing that particular piece. It is not unusual
to find that the child has learned some of the pieces
on his own. Teachers recognize the "magic" of the
first book and use it as a way of establishing a special bond between himself and the pupil.

There are certain considerations in making the
selection of the first book or "primer". It should
be a "special" book, well-crafted with good presentation of musical ideas. Drawings and pictures can be
used in the book, but they should be simple and to
the point. Illustrations should create a mood to get
across a teaching point, but should not be overwhelming. Drawings should be attractive, but not more important than the substance of the book.

Some primers are the first of a long series of
graded books, developed according to the pedagogical
philosophies of the teacher-composer. Many of these

are filled with drawings, charts and instructions for the teacher plus instructions for the pupil, reviews and reminders, and exercises in preparation for the piece (which may be only 4 to 8 measures long). Far preferable is a clean, spacious, simple book. The editor's or composer's directions for the teacher belong in a separate volume or in the preface.

An important quality for a first piano book is its size. The book should be half the standard height of the usual music book. If the book is too tall, the child will have to hold his head in a very uncomfortable manner (especially if it is a grand piano and the child is small). The book also should open easily, be well-bound and printed on heavy quality paper (to stand up to lots of use).

The primer should contain solid musical principles with realistic ideas about playing the instrument. The pieces should make musical and pedagogical sense and should explore the world of music making and develop a freedom of the use of these ideas. This is of prime importance because at this stage the gifts of discovery can be truly exciting for a child. Very first impressions, when received with love and enthusiasm, last forever.

Musical details which the book should include are: dynamics, accidentals, varied time signatures, some key signatures and phrasing. A piano primer should not feature pieces that are all in G clef nor should all pieces center around middle C. The numbers for fingering should be indicated, but not excessively.The child should not be guided by numbers; he should learn to read notes. There are no masterpieces written for beginners; however, the book should set high musical standards.

What if a parent realizes that the child's primer includes all of the things that have just been criticized? First, remember that these comments, though personal opinion, come from years of experience with

hundreds of beginning young students. If a child has
a really good teacher, that teacher will make any
primer work. The good teacher will not depend on
books alone; the book is simply a teaching aid.

Musical Literature

The first years of lessons are the formative ones.
During those years, the child should be exposed to a
wide range of musical literature. Along with "choice"
pieces that should be perfected, there should be a lot
of other music he can "read", providing that the problems in them have been properly solved before he moves
on. There is nothing so devastating to a child as the
feeling that he is "stuck" on the same piece forever.
If the child works hard on the "choice" piece, he
should still have a series of other pieces and exercises which expand his musical experience, reading and
technique. The choice of elementary repertoire is e-
normous and limitless for the piano, but more limited
for the other instruments.

The teacher should not assign the child a thick
book containing pieces in many styles and grades of
difficulty. To the child it conveys the feeling that
this book is going to take a long time to get through.
It is better to present the child with three or four
small books containing several pieces. An example of
a good assignment would be: an important piece of the
repertoire; a book of technical exercises; a duet book;
and a graded book of pedagogical pieces. The goals of
the important repertoire piece are: performance and
expansion of musical content and technique. This piece
will take a longer time to prepare and the student
might spend several months with it. The graded pedagogical pieces have a more immediate goal - a building
of skills and imparting general information. The child
might spend only two weeks on a piece. In addition, a
theory workbook (with exercises to be done at home)can
be used to expand the child's knowledge of music. A
very important book which is often overlooked is a
small notebook to be used as an assignment book. This

is an important teaching tool and link between the teacher, child and parent. The teacher uses it to write notes and advice about pieces being studied, names of new music to be purchased, and other important information.

Responsibilities of the Parent

From the moment that lessons begin, the parent has certain responsibilities. She should make certain that the child goes to each lesson and that he gets there on time. (This might mean the mother, or father, has to spend time driving or walking with the child to the lesson if there is a great distance involved.) When the teacher assigns new music, the parent should help the child get to the music store to buy the music promptly. Just paying for the lessons is not a sufficient commitment on the part of parents if the lessons are to be successful. The child needs to have the feeling that the parents care and that they feel the lessons are important. If the child has difficulty with the teacher and the parents believe that it is a case of the wrong "chemistry" between the two, then it is the parent's task to find another teacher.

At home, the parents should help the child by setting aside a regular practice period so that there is agreement and knowledge that the practice will be daily. If the practicing is something that the child knows he must do, as part of his daily routine, it will help him develop a sense of duty and responsibility with the result that he will argue less about it.

There should be a specific place for practice, away from the rest of the family, the television, and the telephone. Everyone else in the house should respect the privacy of the child by not interrupting the practicing. Some children divide their time and do part of the practice before school and part of the practice after dinner. The parent should help the child find an appropriate time and then help him stick

with it. In addition to a quiet place for practice,
it is important to have a good source of light, and
a comfortable place to sit. For both pianists and
instrumentalists, it is important that the feet be
supported instead of dangling. A box or stool can
be used for support. For pianists, it is extremely
important that the chair be the proper height or else
the hands and arms will not be in the proper position.
If the chair is too low, the elbow will be below the
wrist. If the chair is too high, the forearm will
not be parallel to the floor. For instrumentalists,
a music stand is a must. A bed or table should not
be used as a substitute for a music stand. The stand
is a reasonably priced but essential piece of equipment for the young musician.

When lessons first begin, it is important, particularly with the younger children, that the parent
be physically present during the practice session at
home. The parent's presence signal to the child that
practice is considered important. If the child has
trouble in the beginning lessons, the parent, even
if not musically trained, may still be useful. (In
the Glossary, we have included some musical terms and
information that could be of help to non-musical parents during the beginning lessons.) Beginning lessons
are usually not that difficult to understand.

One of the authors found that when her three
children were beginners they would practice longer
and more happily if she remained in the same room,
knitting. Most of the time, the children ignored her
presence and sometimes they asked questions, most of
which she was unable to answer. She found that many
times while the children were trying to explain to her
what they didn't understand, they found the solution
on their own. By staying close at hand, offering an
encouraging word now and then, or serving as a sounding board for questions, she helped alleviate some
of the frustrations which young children experience
when they are trying to learn something new. Since
learning to play an instrument can be a very lonely

64

experience, a parent's presence in the room can help avoid that.

On the other hand, when supervising the practice session, parents should not oversee so firmly that the child never gets a chance to explore the music on his own. The goal of music lessons is to develop autonomy in practice and learning. By taking all of the responsibility, the parent prevents the child from acquiring that independence. Also, the overbearing parent takes a lot of joy out of exploring and learning music for the child.

If the parent does insist on correcting or criticizing a child's playing, she must explain or analyze her criticisms to the child so that the child can learn something from the comments.

A parent should take care not to issue directions that are contrary to what the music teacher gives. If the parent disagrees with what the teacher says, she should take it up with the teacher privately so that the child is not caught in the middle. If the parent disagrees with the choice of music, it is better to speak to the teacher instead of telling the child he should practice the Beethoven and to ignore the Bartok!

The parent should not punish the child for not meeting the parent's expectations during a practice session. A parent who is a beater not only abuses and damages the child, but also may make the child hate or abandon music. Most parents do not go to such extremes, but some abuse their children verbally by belittling the playing or making negative or disparaging comments.

Some parents want to come to the child's lesson, too. There are no hard and fast rules here, but the main thing to keep in mind is whether the parent is simply observing or whether the parent's presence in the room is having any bad effects on either the teacher or the child. Some children are bothered by having the parent sit through the lesson, as are some teachers. Some children, however, need the security of having the parent there. And some teachers find it helpful if the parent assumes some responsibility in communicating information from the lesson.

If a child is learning to play a wind or string instrument,he has the additional frustration of making the sound as well as tone quality or pitch. The beginning trombonist usually sounds like an elephant in pain, a beginning saxophonist like a sick goose.String beginners produce eery and scratchy sounds and squeaks. If the family complains or laughs at the beginning instrumentalist, he may want to stop. Instead,encourage the child to produce a recognizable tune and when he does, praise him lavishly.Being able to play "Twinkle, twinkle, little star", no matter how many mistakes are made, can prove to be the turning point for a child.

Once the child is able to play simple tunes and read music, he may be ready to accompany singing or play in a group. Since many elementary schools do have instrumental programs and school bands, this makes a very natural and attractive goal for the child because, as one ten-year old observed, "When you play in a group, nobody hears your mistakes. The group covers up your playing." Actually, the feeling of musical community and comradeship is what the child gets from the group. Of course, as the child progresses and begins to outgrow the group, he will need to move on to a more advanced group. Finding such a group (which will probably be outside the school) should be the responsibility of the parent.

When parents are amateur or professional musicians, a special situation exists. There are both benefits and dangers to this situation although the benefits far outweigh the dangers. A child whose parents are musical has the advantage of being brought up in a household that has music as part of its daily life (like eating, brushing teeth, or shopping). A child doesn't need to explain or justify his love or interest in music to such a family. In such a family, the child will be exposed to music without even trying. Parents who have had musical training are more apt to make wiser decisions with respect to the choice of teacher or the music school. A musical parent can do much of the early training in music, introducing the child to the symbols and language of music even before the child has formal lessons. The musical parent is available to help and encourage in the daily practice sessions. (After all, the teacher only sees the child once a week.) Because the musical parent understands the need for silence and discipline if music is to be learned, she will make sure the child practices away from the distractions of the rest of the family and of the television. The musical parent is also helpful in providing activities which result in musical growth, such as concert-going, recordings, and the ability to express musical ideas verbally and through performance. She also has a knowledge of progress or what might be lacking.

On the other hand, the musical parent must be careful about the negative effects her musicality can have on his child. Sometimes if the parent's ambition exceeds that of the child, the parent may try to force the child to achieve something that he cannot do. Such a parent may forget the child in her fixation on achievement so that she disciplines the child or forces him to practice, forgetting that her love for the child and the art of music should take priority over achievement. Because such a parent has musical knowledge, she may be more critical or harsh on the child. She should remember to offer suggestions in a positive way, so that the child does not wind up feeling in competition with the parent or inferior to the parent. As we have mentioned before, an area of potential conflict is the authority of the teacher. The musical parent may give directions to the child contrary to what the teacher has suggested. This challenges the authority of the teacher and puts the child in the middle. It is better to talk to the teacher about this. Overly ambitious parents can cause psychological damage by converting the practice sessions into battlegrounds and the recitals and auditions into torture. If the teacher sees that the parent is creating problems for the child and usurping the teacher's authority, the teacher must speak up. An overly ambitious parent can virtually take over the teaching and cause great psychological damage to the child.

Beginning lessons usually are not too frustrating because of the novelty of the task. Frustration comes when the demands for exacting discipline begin to pile up. Then the parent's task is that of supporting and encouraging the child so that he doesn't quit.

The next crisis comes a few years later at the transition from the childhood to the teenage years. If the child has been studying music for several years already, he has reached the point where the artistic and technical demands of the repertoire become time consuming. It is imperative that the parents get involved at this point if they want a successful transition. If the child can cross the line between the relatively easier repertoire (minuets, sonatinas, etc.) to the more complex and sophisticated repertoire, such as sonatas, concertos, etc., he will have his instrumental skills for the rest of his life.

Making the transition may mean the child has to give up some of his other activities to concentrate his time on developing his musical skills. It takes the same kind of involvement and dedication as that required to become a winner in competitive sports. Unfortunately, in our society it is easier for people to understand the necessity of sacrifice for sports than for music. It becomes all the more important for a child who wants to succeed in music to have the wholehearted support and understanding of his family and his teacher.

INTERMEDIATE AND ADVANCED MUSIC LESSONS

Any book that deals with music must talk about technique and its development. Although some students may never reach the Advanced level (for whatever reasons), the teacher should always keep technique in mind to help the student develop, understand, and perfect what he has learned.

Technique

Technique is a means to an end in music. It is the degree of skills shown in a performance. The great pianist and composer, Sergei Rachmaninoff, believed that technical drill and routine were needed for both student and concert artist. Rachmaninoff practiced scales, trills, chords, octaves and arpeggios because he believed that their mastery was necessary for learning difficult pieces and important in maintaining his pianistic artistry.

In contrast, the famous pianist, Walter Gieseking, believed he needed very little practice because his fingers retained what he learned. In the summer months, he would be away from a piano, yet he could give a concert without difficulty upon his return. He did study new works on the train while traveling between concerts. He felt he did not need much "visible" practice.

Despite the differences of opinions between these two professional pianists, there is some common ground. Both had real and intelligent understanding of the technical passage, in both its musical and physical aspects.

In studying a passage, the student or artist must relate it to the whole, understanding where a particular passage comes from and where it is going next. Once the passage is understood musically, the physical task becomes that of finding the easiest and most natural way of getting from one point to another in terms of preparation, fingering and movement. This probably sounds like an oversimplification but technique is partly a state of mind. Probably facility and ease are comprised mostly of mental attitude and to a lesser degree physical dexterity in the fingers and hands.

The young musician should make a habit of working on technique from the very first lessons because the early years are formative in terms of developing good habits, forming and shaping a hand that is growing,and exploring all the possibilities of the instrument. The role of technique reminds us of the doctor's proverbial little black bag which he carries with him on visits. The doctor looks at the patient, thinks about what he might need and reaches into his black bag for the proper equipment. The musician's black bag is his experience, both musical and technical. There he finds his scales, arpeggios, trills, octaves, chords, etc. There is really no way of side-stepping technique; it is a basic tool and should be taught from the very beginning lesson. Rachmaninoff pointed out that many people believe it doesn't matter what kind of teacher the child starts with. However, he felt that a child with musical aptitude, no matter how young, should start with the very best of teachers. Since first impressions are long lasting, any poor teaching will have to be undone later.

We, too, believe that the first teacher is the one who plants and nurtures the student's attitude about technique. The first teacher is rarely given the credit deserved. If the teacher is good, then he is the most influential teacher in a performer's career.

A good teacher will present technique in a musical and interesting way, making sure that the students know what they are doing and why they are doing it; technique does not have to be "tedious and boring" because it will become a meaningful and exciting process.

70

There are many aspects of technique and we will list and describe several. Because of the authors' backgrounds, many of the examples are pianistic. However, most of them are applicable to other instruments.

It is important to develop sightreading abilities. The better and faster a student can read, the quicker his learning process becomes. He should not watch his fingers when playing, but should look at the music in order to develop a tactile feel for the instrument. Chords (on the piano) and double stops (on strings), leaps and skips and intervals should be played without watching the fingers.

In practicing, the student should never play without conscious thought, repeating the passages and expecting things to happen without trying. Instead, each repetition should be intelligent and analyzed with the goal in mind. If this is done, it may take only 15 minutes rather than one hour to solve a problem.

Fingerings should be thought out rather than improvised each time a piece is played. After carefully analyzing the passage and reaching a decision, fingerings can be written directly on to the music. (This applies mostly to piano, and to a lesser extent, to other instruments.)

Scales should be beautifully played with an even sound despite the fact that fingers are physically disparate (different lengths, strengths and widths). The student can learn to know his own hand and by consciously listening learn to create a beautiful and even sounding scale. Beautiful arpeggios and trills can be developed in the same manner. He can concentrate on sound and technique without worrying about a piece. He can let his imagination go, be creative in the dynamics, different touches, rhythms, developing speed and control and at the same time learning about and observing his arm, elbow, wrist, etc. After a particular execution is finished, the student should have the peaceful and relaxed feeling that comes from

71

a passage correctly played.

Etudes can serve a similar purpose. There are
thousands of etudes written by composers such as
Czerny, Tausig, and others whose main claim to fame
lies in these etudes. While some teachers prefer to
develop technique through concert repertoire, others
use etudes and drills as an independent way of solv-
ing technical problems. The etude can be used as a
week-long sightreading assignment to help reading,and
introduce the pupil to different problems in technique each week. The etude does not have to be played up to the tempo marked in the book, but the reading
must be totally accurate. The etude should be studied
and discussed for its technical content.

At the lesson, the young musician should be learning how to practice. When he goes home, he will try to
recall and to recreate the experience of the lesson.
The teacher will probably advise him to play slowly in
order to become secure in reading the music, fingering,
memorization, rhythm and articulation. However, the
pupil should be listening to what he is playing. He
should be aware of whether the physical approach he
uses when he plays slowly is the same one that he
uses when he speeds up. If it isn't, then the work
has been futile.

A good tip for locating a technical difficulty is
to play a passage quickly first. In doing so,the student will find out exactly where the difficulty is.
After locating the difficulty, the student then pro-
ceeds to work out that section.

If the act of playing music produces pain or tension, the student must be doing something wrong. Music should not require physical pain!

It is helpful.for the young musician to sing a
phrase, watching the dynamic indicators and noticing
where his breath runs out and why. He should correct
the singing then, and afterwards play it on his instru-

72

ment, listening carefully as he plays to see if the instrumental version matches his corrected singing version.

It is useful to memorize a difficult passage because sometimes a problem is caused by trying to look at both the music and the hands at the same time. A passage learned should also be a passage memorized.

The child should avoid mannerisms in playing. Mannerisms can make a child look better than he sounds, or conversely, defeat the effect desired in the passage or prove distracting to the audience.

The student should be taught to end a phrase, to breathe and then to start the next phrase. Tension and stiffness occur when the child is worrying about the next phrase or the next page before he gets there. If the passage has been thoroughly studied as to preparation, execution and release, the playing will be much better. The young musician must pay attention, using his intellect, rather than relying on his musical talents, raw instinct and emotion to carry him through a passage.

Performances, Competitions and Auditions

In addition to technique, the student's music education in the intermediate or advanced stage can include public performances, competitions and auditions. In addition, he may enroll in music courses such as theory, harmony, composing, and conducting. The child may want to join a chamber group, ensemble or advanced orchestra or band. He may also want to begin to play a second instrument.

The teacher can be helpful to the student by seeing that he has an opportunity to perform publicly. The benefits to the student include musical growth and learning to share his music with others, as well as gaining confidence in himself. A performance results in musical growth because the student broadens

73

his technical and musical scope. To play a piece in public, the student may have to memorize the piece and master it at his present level of ability. This gives him a feeling of security and mastery in the music so that nothing upsets his concentration or performance. Usually, the teacher will choose a performance piece that is a little below the child's technical and musical level.

Performing in public is an experience of sharing. Because music is a means of communication, a child who plays only for himself is missing out on something. Children enjoy hearing other children play music.They usually relate the playing they hear to their own. The performance gives them a stimulus for practicing and getting ready to perform, too. The child tells himself, "If my friend can play that music, so can I." If the child hears his piece performed by an artist, he will have a marvelous experience. The performance can provide a glimpse of some hidden beauty in the music and a high standard toward which to aim.

Performance in the arts has a special value, too, because the communication expresses traits and characteristics of the inner self which may never be expressed in any other way. Some children change their personalities when they perform; shy and withdrawn children may be able to express themselves exuberantly. The performance exhibits an aspect of the child that is not evident in the lessons. In contrast to the lesson, the performance is totally outside the teacher's control and adds a new dimension to his understanding of the pupil.

The rewards of performing are numerous. The child who is able to go before an audience, perform the music (no matter how simple or slight) has a feeling of accomplishment. This feeling of accomplishment is present even if the child makes mistakes, but is able to get through the performance. The student who gets flustered, forgets the music, and leaves the stage in tears, will try again, eventually succeeding - if the

74

experience has been discussed and placed in its proper perspective.

After performing, the child receives applause, an indication of the pleasure he has given to his audience. Mostly the audience will be composed of other children, parents and friends, so that the audience will be positive, friendly, sympathetic and appreciative of the child's accomplishment, bolstering the child's confidence and making him want to perform again.

The child who has performed many times will gain a certain self confidence as well as a critical judgment about his own playing. He will know when he has performed up to his level or capability, when he has made mistakes, how he has covered them up, whether his performance is sincere or fake, whether the audience is attentive, etc. There is a benefit in discussing the performance after it is finished, to learn from it and to put it into proper perspective.

The ability to sustain the attention of the audience is also an important reward of performing. Egos need some "stroking" and this is a very positive way of gaining attention. The child's obvious enjoyment of music and his capacity to transmit his joy to the audience will help sustain attention. Mastery of the piece is of paramount importance for sustaining the interest of the audience.

The opportunity to perform in front of an audience provides a goal for the child as far as control and discipline go. If he does it successfully, the performance provides a "stamp of approval". The child who has performed successfully enters a higher and more sophisticated repertoire with self assurance. The good performance expands his ability and serves as a "growing" experience.

At some point the intermediate or advanced student should become involved in competitions for prizes or to play a concerto with an orchestra, etc. This should be a part of a teacher's long-range instruction plan. For some young musicians, the experience of competing is enough; they assess the competition as having been a good experience and an end in itself. Others consider competitions as a challenge and a goal. Still others are smitten with the desire to become "winners". That particular group should be handled with care. The teacher must be careful not to inflate or deflate their dreams. The teacher's task becomes one of helping the student be realistic and in helping the student by listening very carefully... At this point the teacher's work is almost as demanding as the pupil's task!

Competitions can be important. Many musical careers are made by the winning of competitions...as a way of gaining the public's attention.(Van Cliburn's career took a quantum leap after he won the Tchaikovsky competition.) A child who is deeply involved in competitions has to have a deep love for music, a healthy attitude about himself and tremendous drive and endurance. It is impossible for every person to win every competition he enters. There are many heartbreaks and disillusionments. A child whose energy is focused on competitions has to sacrifice all other aspects of his life and concentrate solely on musical development and training. A competition may take a whole year of time to prepare - which is valuable time at such a young age. A young musician should not embark on this path unless he is cognizant of the arduous road ahead and has the strength and talent to endure such a life without becoming bitter towards music.

Stories abound about competitions, how some appear to be fixed, how someone "knew" the judge or sponsor or exerted pressure. Also we must remark that some competitions have forgotten about the artist and have begun to compete as organized events and ends in themselves. However, the majority of the competitions are honorable. Good public relations and pressure on the judges will not help the aspiring winner for very long. In the end it is the public who will really decide whether the student becomes a "star". This is one of the real virtues and saving graces of the arts. The performer who is unable to <u>move</u> audiences, no matter how much publicity or hype has been provided, will not last long in the public's eye.

One of the authors had the task of managing a youth orchestra. At auditions the <u>parents</u> were more nervous and worried than the children. Sometimes that nervousness transferred itself to the children. Parents would do well to ask themselves, does my child want this or do I want this for him? Some parents build up hopes so high that they make their children feel guilty if they fail. The wise parent will help the child evaluate his preparation and performance against the child's own standards of performance. "If you were satisfied that you tried your best and played as well as you could, then it doesn't matter whether you won or lost." Competitions and auditions can be a growing and maturing experience for the child, helping him to learn to judge himself and to measure his progress against what he has been able to do in the past. If the child learns to do this, a giant step forward has been taken.

In auditions for openings in orchestras or bands, the competition may be statewide; each applicant may play the same piece and be judged on his performance. Sometimes, there are little or no seats or openings for the particular instrument that the child plays; this can be disappointing for the child. Auditions should be considered valuable learning experiences, a chance to be judged, but not the "end of the world" if a place in the group is not obtained.

A very important piece of advice for the young performer who is ambitious about auditions and competitions is to be very realistic about the competitiveness of the world he is entering. He should be fully prepared and equipped with a solid knowledge of music history, theory, harmony, counterpoint, and performance practices.

Editions

As the student reaches the level where he starts playing standard repertoire, the teacher will begin to think about assigning a particular edition of the music. Musicians are becoming more edition - conscious thanks to the scholarship of musicologists and artists such as Sir Donald Tovey, Ralph Kirkpatrick, Daniel Pinkham, Paul Badura-Skoda and Howard Ferguson. Many new advances in science and technology (such as the use of microfilming) have resulted in greater access to the original music. The establishment of Musicology Departments and Collegiums of Early Music in our major universities and conservatories have created a demand for good, reliable editions! Gone are the days when a student went to the music store and bought the only edition, albeit a poor one, of the music.

Along with the change in the quality and the quantity of editions available, there has been an increase in the cost of most music editions. However, if the student buys a whole collection of sonatas, preludes, etudes or pieces, instead of the single piece assigned by the teacher, he will have a good edition in his library for many years of service.

Despite their greater cost, the best editions are clean and readable, with pedalling, fingering, dynamics and phrasing faithful to the original manuscript. Some of the cheaper editions have either added notes or omitted phrasing and dynamics.   For a young student, picking an edition that is faithful to the original would be wisest. However, a more advanced student could learn something by looking at other editions such as the Schnabel edition of Beethoven's Sonatas which includes all of Schnabel's ideas about pedalling, fingering and phrasing.   Although these changes are supported by good explanatory notes by the editors and publishers, it is confusing to the young pianist. ·In the preface to this edition, Artur Schnabel, the editor, wrote that he had changed accents and slurs as well as indications of touch . He had abbreviated, added and interpreted the music,without noting all of the changes on the music. He felt that he was musically justified in using his judgment as an artist and musician. Even with all the changes, the Schnabel edition is important because it presents the student with a great artist's views on Beethoven; however, we would not recommend it as the edition to start with.

Besides various editions of music, there are also simplified versions of many pieces. We feel that it is always better to provide a student with an original piece, even if it seems very simple, rather than assigning a simplified version or a transcription. The simplified version is a violation of the composer's intent.

The Metronome as a Learning Aid

The metronome is a mechanical device that marks time with a steady beat, but can be adjusted to beat at a faster or slower speed. The metronome was invented in 1816 by J. N. Mälzel; it is a pyramid-like wooden box equipped with a rod which clicks as it oscillates from side to side. The speed of the clicks can be varied by moving a weight up or down the length of the rod. The rod is graded from 40 to 208, each figure indicating the number of beats per minute. A marking of M. ♩ = 80 means that a quarter note receives one beat, or that there are 80 quarter notes per minute. The metronome indicates the composer's intent as to the pace of the music.

Recently, electronic metronomes have been developed. They use electric clockwork mechanisms and the user varies the speed by changing the settings on the dial.

Music teachers are not in general agreement about the metronome; many pianists and music teachers believe strongly in its value; while some regard it as a useless gadget. We believe that it can be useful, provided that its limitations and its proper uses are clearly explained by the teacher and understood by the pupil.

Practicing exclusively to the beat of a metronome is not advisable for two reasons: the metronome is very anti-musical and also it may make a student learn to depend on it instead of developing his own sense of rhythm. Music, like talking or singing, must have some space to breathe, a space to begin and end a phrase. This cannot be done while playing to the beat of a metronome. Playing along with the metronome completely eliminates the ritardandos,the accelerandos,the sustaining of a note, or the artistic shaping of a phrase, the subtle rubatos or other musical details that a great artist uses to send shivers up the spines of his audience.

The metronome is used to establish the tempo of a piece in accordance with the marking indicated by the composer: for example, Allegro, Andante, Presto, etc. Even though the speed is indicated by using a word, Presto, that word covers a speed anywhere from 100 to 152 (where a quarter note gets one beat). Although the metronome was invented in 1816, not all composers of the day used it. We may find music written before 1816 with metronome speeds written in later by the publisher or the editor. For example: The Bach Prelude no. II from the Well Tempered Clavichord, Book I, was marked ♩ = 144 (vivace) by Czerny (Czerny's rhythm came from his notes on Beethoven's playing). However, tradition and musical sense would give it a Moderato marking.

The metronome can be used to help solve problems for the student. If the student tends to rush or play unevenly, playing along with the metronome can help him learn control so that he pays attention to details of dynamics and uses his fingers evenly. In assigning a new piece to such a student, the teacher can tell him to practice at a slow setting. For example, if

the piece is marked ♩ =168, he can begin the piece
at the pace of ♪ =168, or at half speed. On the
other hand, the metronome can help the student develop
speed in certain passages. This must be done carefully so as not to create tension caused by the challenge
of the prescribed tempo.

The metronome can also be useful to students when
performing a classical sonata. The piece can be given
a feeling of unity, by setting the metronome so that
the subdivisions of the beat permit the player to do
all the movements with a common pulse. The metronome
also helps a student to understand and establish group-
ings of notes within a beat - for example, playing a
quintuplet within a 4 beat measure. In a similar way,
the metronome can help small children understand the
triplet ♩♩♩ (3) .

The metronome is a valuable device for the student in many ways, but should always be considered as
only an aid.

The Tape Recorder as a Learning Aid

Tape recorders, particularly cassette recorders,
are now available at a reasonable cost for relatively
good sound reproduction. The piano reproduces satis-
factorily on almost any recorder, but tone quality
will not be as good for most other instruments on an
inexpensive recorder. However, everything else such
as dynamics, rhythm, notes, etc. will reproduce. It
is with these details that the student is most con-
cerned.

The main value of the recorder is that it gives
the student an opportunity to hear his playing objec-
tively so that he becomes aware of details such as his
phrasing, tempo, clarity, interpretation, dynamics,
etc. Listening to one's playing while performing can
be misleading because the mind supplies things that
are not actually done in the performance. The tape
recorder does not lie. Parts of the performance can

be played back over and over again for listening. By taping a performance, the teacher and his student will be able to discuss it in detail. The tape recorder is also useful in listening to group playing, allowing the pinpointing of difficulties.

Undoubtedly other uses will be found; we have seen students use the tape recorder as an accompaniment for practicing. One child we know uses it to tape a piano accompaniment for his clarinet concerto so that he may practice at home without his accompanist.

* * * * * * * * *

At the intermediate and at the advanced levels of proficiency, sustaining the student's interest and developing his talents and technique are complicated, taxing, though rewarding experiences for both the teacher and the parents. The teacher needs to recognize each child's needs and to prescribe appropriate music and supplementary activities to help the child progress at a happy and comfortable pace. The parent needs to be willing to make a commitment in terms of money, time and support if the child is to reach his full musical potential and be happy about it.

MUSICALLY GIFTED CHILDREN:IDENTIFYING AND HELPING THEM

All children who delight in music lessons, make good progress, and show an avid interest in music are blessed with a "musical gift". However, there are some children who have such an overwhelming interest and talent for music that they fall into a very special category. These "musically gifted" children have special attributes which are of great help to their progress in music,but at the same time create special problems and delights for the teacher and parents. A "musical gift" is such a precious commodity that it ought to be developed to the fullest. However, at the same time,adults should be careful not to exploit the child in the process.

Studies of mature virtuoso performers and composers show that many of them were musical prodigies with extraordinary musical gifts at a very early age. Mozart began concert tours at the age of six when his father began to exhibit him as a prodigy. His compositions at an early age were even more astonishing.At the age of eleven he had composed both symphonies and operettas. By the time he was 14, his opera had been produced. Mendelssohn began to study composition at age eight. That same year he appeared in a concert with two adult horn players. By 15 he had written and produced two operettas. Yehudi Menuhin made his debut on violin at seven and was a celebrity by the time he was eleven years old.A famous composer and conductor, Gunther Schuller,was principal horn player of the Cincinnati Symphony Orchestra by the time he was 18 years old.Lorin Maazel was ten when he conducted Toscanini's NBC Symphony. When he stepped up to the conductor's podium, the musicians sucked lollipops and played wrong notes. He calmly corrected them because he had the entire score in his head.

Although not all gifted children go on to become mature and outstanding artists, many of them do. It would be a pity to waste valuable time in childhood by not providing them with appropriate lessons and

a supportive environment in which to develop their
precocious and unusual gifts!

Characteristics of the Gifted

Are there some special characteristics which distinguish a child with a "musical gift" from an average
child? Some of the more obvious characteristics of
musical talent are: fineness of pitch discrimination,
sense of rhythm,tone quality, understanding of dynamics and interpretation, grasp of chord structure, and
musical memory. Of course, not every gifted child has
every one of these characteristics and each child pos-
sesses these traits in varying degrees.

In general, music teachers who work with gifted
children report that they have some or all of the following characteristics. They are able to accomplish
more work at a faster pace than children of average
musical ability. A gifted child may need to be shown
an example just once,or perhaps,just a few times, before he understands the concept and can reproduce it.
(A less musical child may need to have the explanation
repeated several times before he grasps it.) Music may
be memorized and learned by the gifted child without
an apparent or conscious effort to memorize.

Some musically gifted children can hear a chord
as a unit. Such a child will listen to the bass or
harmony of a piece and be able to reproduce it instantly. An average child might hear the chord, then
analyze it into its components, and then name it
(thinking "c major triad", "c" "e" "g").But the gifted
child skips over that stage; the chord is heard as a
unit in his mind and he does not have to break it down
or "translate" it to reproduce it. A study of composers who were child prodigies showed that most demon-
strated precocity with an outstanding ability to reproduce music precisely after hearing it. They also
experimented with chords. and tunes.Another trait possessed by many is absolute pitch (the ability to reproduce a given note on pitch, after it is named or

heard). These children also discriminate between notes played on pitch or off pitch. While some gifted children are born with absolute pitch, other gifted children have relative pitch (the ability to recognize or reproduce the pitch of a note if it is played immediately after a reference note such as middle C.) Absolute pitch is a particularly helpful attribute for singers, instrumentalists and music teachers. (Studies have shown, however, that pitch discrimination ability can be improved through training.)

There are also variations of absolute pitch ability. A child may only have absolute pitch for one particular piano, or for one particular kind of instrument. The same note played on another instrument sounds different to him. Having absolute pitch (and the ability to recognize a note regardless of the instrument upon which it is played) can be of great help...or hindrance to a musician. Having the ability is useful for transposing music at sight (by thinking of the note as concert pitch and then making an instantaneous transposition). Such a gift allowed one child to play saxophone (without having lessons) on the basis of his clarinet playing. On the other hand, transposed music sounds "wrong" to a child with absolute pitch. Such a child will have difficulty in playing an instrument that is out of tune. It is said that Mozart was bothered by notes pitched one-quarter tone off.

Not all gifted children have absolute pitch, but it is of help to those children who want to play any instrument which requires the ability to hear the exact sound (strings, trombone, or to a lesser degree, the woodwind instruments and drums). Absolute pitch is also of great help in conducting because conductors can hear keenly all the various instruments in the orchestra as well as transpose the written score into sound.

Many gifted young children seem to be able to play music beyond what one would normally expect for their age. They are able to "leap" around the instrument, finding the right notes even if they are playing a very complicated piece of music. They seem to be able to play music that physically ought to be impossible for them to do. Many musically gifted children also seem to be brighter than average. Studies of the gifted have shown them to be above average in health, strength and physical development when compared to average children. Along with their ability to produce music above what would be expected at their age level, these children may have the ability to synthesize music from the written page, grasping it as a whole by sight and in their minds, and then reproducing it on an instrument. Some gifted children can "h e a r" the music while looking at the notes on the printed page. A four-year old girl was able to sing, on pitch, music that she saw for the first time. A more extreme example was the composer Saint-Saens who could reduce a complicated orchestral score on sight and play it instantly on the piano.

Many of the gifted memorize quickly and effortlessly, retaining the music in their minds for a long time. Walter Gieseking, a noted pianist, memorized all of Beethoven's Sonatas at the age of 15 and played them in six recitals. Since putting the finishing touches on music depends on memorization, such children have a great advantage over other children who must memorize music note by note which is a slow painstaking process. The child with a good musical memory probably conceptualizes the music in terms of chords, harmonies, and other musical ideas; some children are able to listen to the radio or to a record and then reproduce the sound on an instrument without having to use written music.

Memorizing quickly or instantaneously can create some problems. A child who memorizes wrong notes or forgets to study the dynamics of the piece before he memorizes it, will have trouble. An occasional child who has a "good ear" may fail to learn to read music because it is easier for him to learn everything by ear.

Another characteristic that many gifted children possess is a strict sense of rhythm. Such a child will notice the difference between music played in different rhythms such as 3/4 or 4/4 because the piece "sounds" different to him. A child with a good sense of rhythm can accurately keep the beat internally so that he does not shift rhythms. This innate sense of rhythm is particularly helpful if he wants to play in a chamber music group or conduct. A child with a good sense of rhythm can automatically divide and subdivide the measure in his head, correctly performing sixteenth notes and thirty-second notes, for example.

Another useful attribute possessed by the gifted child is an intuitive knowledge of fingerings, or at least an ability to develop a quick "muscle" knowledge of correct fingerings so that it is not necessary to keep thinking about them or looking them up. This learning is almost instantaneous in some children. Most prodigies also have no difficulty in mastering technicalities of their chosen instrument because they have good small motor coordination.

In addition to an excellent ear, instant memory, thinking in terms of chords, strict sense of rhythm, good pitch discrimination and good small motor coordination, a truly musically gifted child has one other area in which he excels - a discriminating taste or special feel for the beauty of sound. This enables the child to see the melodic line as a whole, rather than having to learn the music note-by-note and then attempting to put it together.This quality of "interpretation" brings meaning and beauty to a phrase. It is the difference between the music of an artist and that of a perfect "technician". The technician can do a perfect and literal rendering of the music, but the artist imbues the sound with a meaning that transcends the actual notes. This ability to interpret is not learned, although it can be refined through teaching. Such talent allows a child to pick up a piece of music he has never seen before and perform it, making good sense of it,and bringing out its intrinsic beauty.

Guiding the Gifted

Because gifted children have some or most of the characteristics mentioned above, their progress in music is often phenomenal. They may cover in one year what another child of the same age may take two or three years to learn. Sometimes what they can do in their minds leaps ahead of what they are able to accomplish with their fingers. As parents and teachers, we owe these gifted children special consideration. Because they do make rapid progress, it is often a temptation to let them move ahead rapidly without giving them time to consolidate and refine what they have learned. Music teachers should be particularly careful to avoid any shortcuts to learning. These children must be provided with a "full diet" of music including technical exercises, and pieces that on the surface appear deceptively easy, but can be played at many different levels of accomplishment.

While trying not to push the child too rapidly ahead, the teacher should avoid making the opposite mistake. The solution is to provide him with a wide variety of different kinds of music and musical experiences at his level while giving him some music just above his reach. This will satisfy both the short term and long term goals. The same approach should be taken with the gifted child as with the average child; however, with the gifted child, the whole learning process is telescoped. Some child prodigies who started musical training late accomplished a tremendous amount in just two to four years. Aaron Copland started piano at 14 and already knew he would be a composer at 16. Dmitri Shostakovich started lessons late, at nine years old, because his mother, a pianist, did not believe in giving lessons before the age of nine. However, by the time he was eleven, he was on his way to becoming a composer.

The parent's role in the gifted child's musical education is a very delicate one. The parents need to be supportive, but at the same time they should not push their child. This is a sensitive task. It would be extremely helpful to stay in good communication with the teacher so that both work together for a common goal --- the benefit of the child.

An example of good parental support is provided by the case of Yehudi Menuhin. His parents created a total environment for Yehudi and his two sisters (who later became concert pianists). The parents were careful not to exploit him, limiting his number of appearances, allowing him to spend the bulk of his time in violin lessons. The parents refused to let him play for Queens or patrons. The family was able to gain support from a wealthy patron so that the whole family was able to go abroad together. The parents regulated the lives of children with lessons, learning of languages, physical exercises, and practice of $2\frac{1}{2}$ to 3 hours per day.

Another very gifted musician and composer, Phillipa Schuyler, made tremendous progress because of the total support of her parents who helped her develop into a person of many talents. Although she performed at important concerts at a very young age, played on national radio at the age of four, and had her compositions performed by orchestras at a young age, there was a normalcy to her life that allowed her to become a talented musician, a gifted journalist, and a humanitarian, by the time she died a tragic and premature death in a rescue mission in Vietnam.

At the other extreme, we have Ruth Slenszynska, a child prodigy who made her piano debut at the age of four. In reminiscing in her autobiography, "Forbidden Childhood", she told about being forced to practice nine hours a day, being slapped and beaten for her mistakes and never being allowed to be a child. At eight she already had three full one-hour concert programs which she played from memory.

The role of the parent in fostering and following

up musical ability and interest at an early age is very important. It would be wonderful if musical talent were spotted at an early age and followed up as in the case of concert pianist, Byron Janis, whose kindergarten teacher remarked to his parents that he seemed quite gifted in picking out tunes on the xylophone.His parents then arranged for him to start piano lessons. In studying the backgrounds of child prodigy composers, we·find that most of them came from homes that were musical or at least supportive and cultural. Although the fathers enjoyed the musical abilities of their sons, most insisted that their sons pursue careers outside of music. In general, it was the mothers who were most supportive and often served as the child's first teacher. In the case of a number of child prodigies who came from culturally deprived and non-musical backgrounds, the church and its music often served the purpose of getting the child interested and launched into the world of music.

If a parent has a child who is musically gifted, what approach should she take? First and foremost,the cues should come from the child himself. Most musical prodigies showed interest in music from a very early age, begging for lessons or for an instrument. Often, the parent started the child on an instrument and the child begged to switch to another instrument of his own choosing. A well-known pianist smashed to bits a violin her father gave her, indicating that it was the piano which she wanted to play. Her father wisely let her learn piano. Violinist Isaac Stern had had two years of piano lessons and was ready to give up when he heard someone practicing the violin and asked to switch.

The parent must decide how much to push or encourage any particular child. The only way that the child is going to make progress is to spend time perfecting his technique...by practicing. Time spent in practicing has to be balanced against school work, time for socializing, sports and other extracurricular activities. Of course, there are individual differences in learning and different children benefit by putting in different amounts of practice time, whether it is done all at once, spread out, long hours, by short intervals, morning, night, etc. Andre Watts, the pianist, put in 6 hours of practice 6 days each week while Arthur Rubinstein, when young, cheerfully endured his hours of practice time by arming himself with a bowl of cherries, a box of chocolates and a good novel.Ruth Slenszynska spent 9 hours a day in practice while Yehudi Menuhin spent 2½ to 3 hours a day.

The parents can be very helpful to the child by discussing priorities with him---musical and otherwise. Some young musicians would rather do average academic work in school while devoting the greater part of their free time to practicing music rather than taking "honors" courses and putting in more time for exams and papers. This is an acceptable path if the parents and child are in agreement on it. Some musically gifted children prefer to excel in school. If the parent recognizes the child's musical talent, and tells him, "You have this talent and you are wasting it by not practicing...", the child will feel guilty. It takes real wisdom and patience on the part of the parents to guide the child to the right course. Of course, the music teacher can provide parents with suggestions, evaluating the talent and providing advice. The music teacher is in the position of knowing what is involved in a career of music; he can present a realistic viewpoint to the parents.

If parents and teachers have a good relationship, they can sit down together and discuss the child's music education with the child's needs in mind. All sorts of considerations should play a part in the decision...what is the child's feeling toward music... is it something he just enjoys, or is he very serious about it? Does the child have other interests and skills that compete with music? Is the child single-minded and dedicated in his approach to music? Is he willing to go through the hard work and sacrifice needed to achieve the heights in music? Parents should realize that work and discipline have no substitutes in the development of talent.

Test of Musical Abilities

We have talked about evidence of musical ability which can be recognized by adults who know the child. When a child enters school, he is tested in different ways for IQ, achievement, etc. One of the tests might be for musical achievement.

There are a number of musical tests available. Each tests different traits of musicality depending on the author's philosophy as to what traits of mucality make up that elusive quality known as "musical ability". We will describe some of the tests briefly and comment on some of the advantages and drawbacks of each test. Tests can be judged on reliability (whether a child who is retested with the same test would get a comparable score the second time),and validity (if test scores are compared with another measure of musical ability such as teachers' ratings,will the results be similar?) Most tests of musical ability are group tests and not individual tests.Although there have been a number of tests of musical ability produced over the years, we will talk only about some of the more familiar standardized tests which are commercially available.

The Seashore Measures of Musical Talents which was first published in 1919 measures native and basic capacities in musical talent before training has begun and it measures one specific capacity at a time. A group test, which was republished in 1960, it has subtests in: pitch, loudness, rhythm, time (recognizing which one of two tones is longer), timbre and tonal memory. The test (which can be given to children aged 10 to adult) involves the use of a beat - frequency oscillator and tuning forks because it was felt that the tests should not be contaminated by factors indigenous to a particular culture. Published by the

Psychological Corporation, the Seashore test takes one hour to administer. Reliability is good, but the validity is lower except for the pitch, rhythm and tonal memory tests.

A second commercially available test is the Kwalwasser-Dykema Music Test. It has several subtests which measure pitch, quality, intensity, tonal movement, time, rhythm, tonal memory, melodic taste, pitch imagery, and rhythm imagery. Used for ages 10 years to adult, it depends on orchestral instruments and a special piano (the Duo Art reproducing piano). The test is published by Carl Fischer and takes one hour to administer. Reliability for this test seems to be lower than the Seashore (judged by independent studies). The validity measures are low, but the test does discriminate between the most musical and the least musical of the group.

The Drake Musical Aptitude Test takes 20 minutes to administer and it tests children beginning at 8 years to musically superior adults. The subjects taking the tests should have had some music lessons; the Drake test is more of an achievement test. The test, which is published by Science Research Associates, has good reliability and validity. Areas tested are memory and rhythm. There are two forms of the test.

The Wing Standardised Tests of Musical Intelligence uses the piano as a stimulus and the content of each subtest is more musical than most tests (familiar melodies are performed). Subtests include chord analysis, pitch change, memory, rhythm, harmony, intensity and phrasing. The ages that can be tested are 8 years to adult. The reliability and validity are good. The test takes an hour to administer and is published by the National Foundation for Educational Research.

The Bentley Measures of Musical Ability consists of four tests: pitch discrimination, rhythm memory, tonal memory and chord analysis. The stimuli used are an oscillator and an organ. The test is planned for age

7 or for ages 8 through 14 years old. Reliability is good and the validity is significant when teachers' judgments of musical ability in several groups of children are compared to test results. The tests take 20 minutes to administer and are published by Harrap.

The value of tests such as these are that they sometimes provide clues as to whether a child can hear different tones, discriminate whether they are higher or lower on a scale, whether a child is able to distinguish grades of loudness and softness or length or brevity of duration of a note. Tests can also provide a picture of the capacity of a child to imitate sounds and rhythms and the ability to store information (his memory). Achieving a high score on all these traits might be ideal equipment for somebody who aspires to become a musician. However, in an average group of children, a surprisingly large percentage might score well. This could happen because musical aptitude tests measure basic abilities that are related to music but are not necessarily musical.

What then are the uses of these tests? One use might be diagnostic. If a child is already taking lessons, but seems to be having trouble, the test might be able to pinpoint the child's difficulty, although an astute teacher ought to be able to figure this out on his own. Tests given before the study of an instrument is begun might be used to help guide the child to choose an instrument that he would be most likely to succeed in playing. Tests might be useful in school situations where the administration wants to pick out a number of children to be given more intensive musical training mostly for the creation of bands, choruses and orchestras. Some schools do not use the standardized tests, but prefer to devise their own.

As we mentioned earlier, most musically gifted children will be noticed by the parents and teachers. Since the music tests rarely are used before the age of 8 (or age 7 in the case of the Bentley Music Test), most musical geniuses have already begun their musical

careers by the ripe old age of 8! It is also our o-
pinion that some of the most musically gifted students
would have flunked the music tests; they may not see
the answers in terms of black and white because they
hear more than what the test is testing, or the child
may not be able to express what he knows, or perhaps,
the child has a slight learning disability.

One of the authors taught a child who could sing
perfectly,but she always sang at a pitch different
from the piece being played. The girl sang an inter-
val of one third above whatever the teacher happened
to be playing. If the teacher switched his piano accompaniment to her pitch, she could continue singing
without difficulty. Eventually, through singing exercises and knowledge of intervals, she overcame her
difficulty. However, had she been tested, she would
have been told that she had a "tin ear" or was "tone
deaf", and she would have been reluctant to sing in
front of anyone or would have forgone the happy experience of learning music. Another child with whom one
of the authors worked, was quite gifted, but backward
in English. The child might have understood or known
the correct answers, but could not have expressed them
in the form that was needed (marking a paper). For him,
knowledge was acquired and transmitted through his
fingers. Since music tests are culturally determined
with "right answers" which depend on knowledge of
Western music, a child who knows modern or contemporary music, might give the "wrong answers". At the same
time, since most of the tests measure qualities that
can be improved through music lessons (understanding
of rhythms, pitch, etc.) the child who has had music
lessons or similar learning experiences would have an
advantage, probably scoring higher than a more gifted
child who had not had such exposure.

At an informal conversation among several musicians, it was discovered that only one had had any
formal testing as a child. That individual came
from New York, a state where there was emphasis on
identifying children gifted in the arts. After she

was tested as a child, the woman's parents were called, and told she should be encouraged to take music lessons. She was put in a group which was given special musical activities. We wonder what happened to those children who were excluded from the musical training. Surely they would have benefitted from many of the special musical activities and demonstrations.

A child who did not score well on just such a group test was later found to be extremely musical by his mother, a musician. She arranged for him to have piano lessons. Because he is gifted, he is progressing very well. There is a danger in depending on such tests for making decisions about any particular child. Tests are best used to provide information on groups of children. No child should be excluded from the experience of music; every child can benefit in some way.

A Plea for the Gifted

We need to single out and support our gifted children. Tremendous amounts of money have been invested in all kinds of programs to help solve the problems of the disadvantaged, but very little has been done to help those individuals who have been born with a special gift. One of the biggest obstacles to promoting the cause of the gifted has been the pervasive belief that it is undemocratic to identify the gifted when they are young. Yet, paradoxically, we reward the best and brightest as adults. By not identifying and helping the gifted when they are young, we let them waste those most important formative years, stagnating in mediocre school systems where the group moves no faster than the slowest child. This hesitancy is caused by the fear of "elitism" and the feeling that the gifted child will "make it" on his own anyway.

Recognizing that the first years of a child's life are extremely important in his development and to help fill the void that exists in education for the gifted, Richard Robbins, the Director of the Music

School at Rivers in Weston, Massachusetts, and one of the authors organized a class for musically gifted five year olds. Children were interviewed and selected for their love of music, musical ear, motor coordination and imagination. With the help of scholarship funding, the children came from all ethnic, economic and social classes.

Classes were held for two hours twice each week. After one year, these children can read music and deal with mathematical concepts involved in rhythm and notation although they have not yet learned math since they are of preschool age. (For an example of teaching children rhythm and notation, see the Appendix.) Although some of them have perfect pitch, those who do not have developed a more acute relative pitch so that their singing is always in tune.

During the second year, some of the children will start learning an instrument and they will also participate in one hour of chorus and one hour of musical skills each week.

There were many reasons for starting this program. We feel strongly that children who are ready for music should not have to wait for instruction until they are much older. The early training gives them a head start to establish their musical skills before they must undergo adjustment to school pressures. These children will start their chosen instruments intellectually and physically ready to absorb and progress at a much faster pace than had they waited until later. Since they all have an avid interest in music, they enjoy exploring music with their peers. Even though they may get involved with other interests outside of music in the future, they have developed an intelligent sensitivity toward music which will stay with them for the rest of their lives.

Just recently, federal legislation recognized this deficiency and created an Office of the Gifted and Talented. State Governments are now beginning to write position papers on the subject suggesting that the gifted be singled out for special attention. It is our hope that early recognition and support of musically gifted youngsters will be a top priority in these programs when they are implemented.

MUSIC FOR SPECIAL NEEDS CHILDREN

This chapter has been one of the most difficult for us to write. Because of our interest and deep involvement with musical achievement for the average and the gifted child, we did not have much information on the role of music in the education of special needs children. When researching this topic, we found that this is a recent issue of great importance to educators, psychologists, and politicians. However, outside of a number of British books written on the subject, we found little published information. As we write this, we realize that there must be a great deal of information being gathered which is not yet available to the general public.

In our belief that music should be accessible to every child, we cannot ignore this exciting and promising facet of music which is rapidly becoming an important national issue. Until very recently most teachers had no experience in working with a special needs child with the exception of the music therapist. Federal legislation and the mandate to "mainstream" special needs children into regular classes and schools make it imperative that we change our attitudes and thinking about what special needs children can, and should be able to,accomplish.

The term "special needs" is extremely broad and can include many types of handicaps: mental, physical and emotional. Some special needs children will achieve a high level of musical accomplishment by compensating for their handicaps.For other special needs children, music can be used as therapy, either physical or psychological.

Finding ways for a child to compensate for a handicap is not particularly difficult. Ruth Edwards, in her book The Compleat Music Teacher describes how her pupil with a short arm experimented until he found the right position at the piano. A student who had lost a leg was taught to use the left leg for pedalling. To compensate for the loss of the use of the soft pedal, he developed his pianissimo technique.

A child who had only one finger on one hand and just two on the other successfully learned to play the trumpet with the aid of a special stand. There are a number of gadgets available which can hold music or instruments so that the child can play even with a handicap.

Some of the piano music for the left hand owes its existence to Paul Wittgenstein, a one-armed virtuoso. The famous violinist Rudolph Kolisch who could no longer use the fingers of his left hand normally, retaught himself to play by using the fingers of the right hand on the strings.

Loss of the use of the legs should not deter the child from a musical career. Most children can still play any instrument that requires only the use of the arms and mouth. Pinkas Zukerman, the violinist who had polio as a child, performs from a chair.

Blind children, although they usually compensate through improving their hearing skills, should be taught to read braille music. The blind pianist, George Shearing, who could play everything by ear, was stymied by Bach fugues. He wanted so badly to be able to play them that he learned Braille music notation in order to do so. If a child has partial sight only, he can use a magnifying glass to read the music.

There has been some music work done with deaf children. Vibrations can be felt and the children can be taught rhythms. A device was recently invented which allows the deaf person to "hear" symphonic music. Although some deaf children have found it pleasurable, no one really knows what it is they are actually hearing.

With the exception of deaf children, we have described ways children with handicaps can learn music. These children are learning music at the highest level to which they can achieve. For some of them, compensatory techniques have allowed the child to achieve at an extremely high level. For others, the achievement may be less, but the music is still at an acceptable level.

Music can also be used for emotional and physical therapy. Ruth Edwards wrote about using music as a tool when she worked with emotionally disturbed hospitalized patients. She used music as a tool or as therapy to reach them. She organized a chorus in which the patients in the hospital were invited to participate. By exposing them to this musical opportunity, she "drew out" many patients. This musical participation had a ripple effect. Once the patient had opened up to music, he then began to be more receptive to change or new experiences in other areas of his life and this often led to progress in the patient's case. Music was used as a means here, as therapy, rather than as an end (achievement).

Music therapy has been used with severely handicapped and emotionally crippled children. In the book, They Can Make Music, Philip Bailey describes various ways in which instruments...xylophones, sound blocks, horns, drums, etc. can be arranged so that the child can be taught to play. The child may play only part of a tune, not even a simple line of melody. The resultant sound is a form of "music" which might not be particularly satisfying to a musician with high standards, but it becomes an effective form of musical therapy in which the children can see progress which then carries over into other areas of their lives. Some musicians find it hard to call this music - because it is gimmicky and full of contraptions. The goal of this music making is the emotional satisfaction and helping of the child, not the production of the highest quality music.

101

Music teachers who work with special needs children must be extremely patient, highly optimistic and hopeful, creative and inventive as they adapt their musical knowledge and technique to the children.Progress with the children may be very slow. Teachers may have to spend countless hours preparing elaborate charts and reports to record the smallest progress. But, when progress does occur, it has a great significance for the child and is very gratifying for the adult working with the child. Although the music produced by these children may not be of the highest artistic quality, for some of these children music may be their first and only form of communication with the rest of the world and gives them their first sense of accomplishment.

In addition to providing emotional therapy for special needs children, music lessons can provide physical therapy. In the case of a child with cerebral palsy who loved music and wanted to play the piano,the child could only play with the fist clenched.The child learned to play with a clenched fist and the teacher helped play the music as a duet. The teacher directed the child's energies toward composing and singing.However, just the fact that the child tried to play the single line of melody was helpful and provided physical therapy and improvement in the hands and fingers. A case in a Suzuki violin class was affected on one side by infantile paralysis. Her coordination was so poor that the violin bow constantly flew out of her grip. Her mother spent most of the first year patiently retrieving it for her. Mother and child had a great deal of patience and stuck with the lessons until the girl eventually improved in both her playing and in the coordination of her left side.

There are many ways in which music can be used with special needs children. In the case where the handicap, whether emotional or physical, is not so severe as to interfere with performance, compensations can be made which will still result in a high level of musicianship. Other children, even though compensating, can still achieve a satisfactory level of musicianship. Music can also be used as both psychological and physical therapy for children with special needs.

A few years ago there was little funding or attention paid to special needs children. It is apparent that big advances have been made, although not nearly enough to solve this complex problem.However we feel that a growing consciousness about special needs is taking place and we cannot help but foresee the tremendous benefits to be gained by the children and by the rest of society.

THE VARIETIES OF MUSIC: FOLK, ROCK, POP, JAZZ AND "CLASSICAL" CONTEMPORARY

We have been talking about music in general, but have not been specific as to the many different kinds of music. Everyone makes his own judgment as to the value of any particular kind. There is room for different types of music in a musical education and its development.Also, musical interests and tastes do not develop in an orderly progression nor in a straight line, but they co-exist. For example, someone who plays classical music might love jazz music.

Folk Songs

Although there are a number of forms of music to which a child might be exposed, one of the easiest ways to interest a young child is by the use of folk songs. The music has direct appeal, the melodies are easy-to-grasp and straight forward, and the harmonies are simple and easy to comprehend. Accompaniment is generally on the guitar or banjo. Children can sing along. With the increased interest in folk songs in the 1950's and the emergence of such master folk artists as Burl Ives, Richard Dyer-Bennett, Pete Seeger, the Weavers, Tom Glazer, Frank Luther, Marais and Miranda, etc., all of whom gave concerts and made records, good folk music became readily available. For adults who have listened only to classical music, folk songs offer a stepping-stone to other kinds of music. Folk music teaches children games, languages, customs, geography, and the history of other cultures.
Many contemporary composers have borrowed themes from folk songs of their native countries. Bartok's Microkosmos, Dvorak's Slavonic Dances, Lizst's Hungarian Dances, Ralph Vaughan Williams' Greensleeves, and the music of Sibelius, Tchaikovsky, Brahms and Kodaly owe some themes to folk songs. These pieces make enjoyable listening because the folk material is recog-

nizable even though it has been transformed by a master composer.

In addition to listening to records and singing along, children also enjoy singing folk songs with an adult. Many adults have mastered a few simple chords on the guitar or on the piano. There is an immediate satisfaction for the child in being able to reproduce what he hears on the record, but in his own individual way. Folk songs usually have strong rhythms, are repetitious and can be adapted for use in musical games; some examples of folk songs which can be used for games are: "She'll Be Coming 'Round the Mountain", "Ring Around a Rosy", "On Top of Old Smoky".

Introducing Classical Music

Parents and classroom teachers should also introduce classical music to children. One of the authors of this book heard recordings of the classics "ever since I can remember. My father used to play his records at night just about the same time I was put to bed; there are certain pieces of music which I knew completely by the age of four. As far as contemporary music went, nothing beyond Rachmaninoff was heard in the house." The other author had a similar experience, hearing only classical piano music as a child. Both authors found their way to contemporary and other kinds of music by chance.

The author who is a musician describes his experience: "My love of Stravinsky began by chance. As a very young boy, I used to save some of my allowance to buy records or new figures for my toy circus. When I was 7 or 8 years old, I bought Stravinsky's 'Rite of Spring' because of its record jacket with a Rousseau painting which absolutely fascinated me. The exotic vegetation, the mysterious lady, the moon, the animals and the bold colors and design were appealing to my childish imagination. When I actually listened to the recording, it completed my world. Even though the music was very different from what I had heard before, I knew these sounds, and I felt the rhythms were real and very natural.

"I did not actually see a score of this piece until I was 18 years old; I could not believe that it was so technically complex and difficult.The purchase of that recording really changed my life. Now when I present contemporary music to my students, I do it without explaining why I am giving it to them. Young minds are flexible and children accept contemporary or new music without prejudice."

The other author was introduced to contemporary music also by chance. "In the 1950's the Chicago Symphony offered 60 cent tickets to students on Tuesdays and Fridays. Whenever I could, I took the IC train from the University of Chicago campus to the Loop to hear a concert. Hearing Respighi's Birds was a revelation to me. In the same period, I also had a chance to watch the Fine Arts Quartet,a string group, perform Ravel's Quartet. Attending live performances made it easier for me to grasp and appreciate the music,which was very different from any music I had ever heard before. From that chance beginning, I was able to go on to enjoy other contemporary compositions."

Children can be introduced to classical music through records, even though music is used informally as background music (without actually sitting the child down and expecting him to listen attentively) and through live concerts, radio and television. It would be best to start with simple piano music or an orchestral piece such as Tchaikovsky's Nutcracker Suite. In the nursery school where she taught, one of the authors used Swan Lake, orchestrations of Bach's Preludes and Fugues, and some Pablo Casals cello recordings as background music for four year olds in the class room. (In the Appendix of this book, we list other recordings which are especially suited for young people's listening.)

Popular Music, Rock and Disco

Some parents and teachers are upset when children begin to listen to the "Top 40" (popular music or rock played on the radio). This is a particularly trying period for those adults who believe that the only good music is classical music. It is helpful for such adults to realize that part of the interest in popular music, rock and disco is <u>social</u>, that the children want to sing, dance, and go to concerts with their peer group. The main advantage of a child listening to the "Top 40" is that he is showing some interest in music; parents and teachers can build from that.

Some pop and rock music has classical roots. In the 1940's, "I'm Always Chasing Rainbows" was based on the music of Chopin. More recently, we have a "Fifth of Beethoven" and the tunes from <u>Kismet</u> based on the music of Borodin. While the metamorphosis of these tunes is not done in impeccable taste, a child who hears the music could be enticed to listen to the original music.

One author's children received an inexpensive tape recorder as a present. Although they were studying classical music, they were fascinated by the music they heard on the radio ("Top 40"). They taped the music they heard, assembling a complete collection of the most popular hit songs on the charts. This interest in popular music was further stimulated by their new piano teacher who had studied classical music, but who was currently studying and composing jazz at Berklee College of Music. The teacher taught the boys how to play chords and the rudiments of jazz and also got them interested in trying to play the "Top 40" music on the wind instruments they were studying in the School Band. The children found the music pleasant, easy to listen to and to play, but after a while, they tired of it. They then started to compose and perform their own popular and jazz music.

Some children become very fascinated by hard rock music. Rock has many of the same qualities as folk music and pop music...catchy tunes and harmonies and lots of repetition. However, there are some differences. The beat is stronger and the identification of the listener with the singer or performer is **greater** because the listener often moves or dances to the music. The listener is encouraged to sing along with rock because the melody is simple and repetitive, the accompanying chords are easy, and the music is so loud and overwhelming that it is impossible to ignore. Rock singers usually do not have trained voices and may yell hoarsely. Almost anyone can sing along, and this increases the appeal. Instrumentation for rock usually includes an electric guitar or two, drums, bass, a singer or singers and synthesizers. Brass and wind instruments or piano are sometimes used in groups (such as the one known as Chicago). Since rock is fairly easy to imitate, the young are quick to form rock bands.

Disco, the newest music fad,appeals to the young because of its steady, dependable beat, the ease of following the music and dancing to it, the constant repetition of phrases, simple harmonies, melody,smoother vocals, and the fact that it is easier on the ears than rock. There are many adaptations of popular tunes and the classics to which the disco beat is added. For older teenagers or young adults, the disco scene is a world in itself...with special clothing, lighting effects, pulsating music and friends moving to the beat. The latest touch added to the scene is roller disco!

Perhaps the main appeal of folk music, "Top 40", rock and disco is the tendency of the music to engage the untutored ear immediately. The music makes the listener feel,"I can do it, too". The appeal draws the youngster toward the music, introducing him to the musical elements of rhythm, structure, harmony, melody. It is difficult for some parents to admit that there is a value in this kind of music and that the child will also reach out to try other kinds of music. Pop, rock, disco and folk music all have the advantage of encouraging the children to explore music, to perform, or even to compose their own music. Once they have started performing, children may involve themselves in more complicated music...orchestral and wind music, jazz, brass and wind trios, quartets, quintets or concertos in both classical and contemporary styles. If children are forbidden to form their own groups to play the music that feels comfortable and natural to them, they may lose their interest in music completely.

Jazz

One other area of music which is a natural progression from the "top 40" is jazz with its improvisation. Unfortunately, the word "jazz" includes much music: from Scott Joplin's Ragtime to the music of artist-composer Dave Brubeck, Charlie Parker (Be Bop), Duke Ellington, Count Basie,etc. to the newest kind - - fusion jazz, Third Stream and avant-garde.To explain all the different kinds of jazz music would fill a book - a recent book on jazz numbered several hundred pages and covered almost as many musicians and their styles. When talking about jazz, even to a jazz buff, attempts to communicate can be difficult, if not impossible.

The many varieties of jazz have certain common characteristics. The rhythm (written down as eighth notes) is played as triplets $\prod = \int_3 \int$. It has a syncopated sound - long followed by short. The chords in a jazz piece tend to be complex and include a lot of sevenths (C, E, G, Bb) or ninths (C, E, G, Bb, D) rather than simple triads (C, E, G). A jazz piece usually takes the form "A A B A" with each section being 8 or 12 measures long. The "A" section is the "head" (or theme) and "B" is the bridge (usually written in a different key). Improvisation can be done at any point throughout the piece. The soloist improvises around fixed or predetermined chords.There

109

is a certain amount of freedom available to the rhythm section - the piano, bass, guitar and drum. While each works from a chart of specified chords, there is variation in each performance because there are not any given notes to be played and nothing is written out.

The concept of improvisation is quite simply "as old as the hills". Concertos written in the time of Mozart, Haydn and Beethoven had a place for a cadenza, a spot or an opportunity for an individual soloist to play unaccompanied and even compose his own passage if he wanted to do so. Often performers played what the composer suggested for that spot or they planned it out and practiced it ahead of time. Some performers approached the cadenza and improvised on the spot, much as a jazz artist does today. There is one difference, however. The jazz soloist stays within the framework of the particular chords he is given.

Improvisation was in common use in the Baroque era. Baroque Chamber music used wind instruments, string instruments, and a harpsichord. Harpsichord music consisted of a keyboard accompaniment of bass notes. The chords to be played in the right hand were improvised, usually with the help of numbers or figures written underneath or above the bass notes (this was called a "figured bass" or "bass continuo"). Details and additions were left up to the player's skill and his ingenuity. This "basso continuo" reminds us of today's "fake book" used by jazz players where the melody has been written out and the bass chords are indicated by chord notation, leaving the player to invert or to improvise on the chords. Jazz has ties to early music; immersion in the study of jazz might lead a young person back in time to the study of early and classical music.

There are many varieties of jazz. Some forms of jazz are "easier" to listen to than others (for example, the music of Duke Ellington or Count Basie). Both use the "Big Band" format with "charts" (arrangements written out); yet they leave room for solo improvisation. A group such as the Dave Brubeck Quartet follows somewhat the same format, but uses only four instruments, i.e., piano, saxophone, bass and drums rather than the 16 instruments which the Big Band sound uses. Brubeck's training was classical and this no doubt influences the music he writes. Other jazz forms include "fusion" jazz which incorporates musical idioms or instruments from other cultures (Indian tabla or African drum, for example) along with more traditional instruments. "Third Stream" jazz creates a blending of jazz and classical elements, using jazz melodies and "spicing" up classical harmonies. "Avant-garde" jazz is free form, somewhat freeing for some listeners, but creating uneasiness in others if they search for structure or closure. A popular exponent of avant-garde jazz is the pianist, Keith Jarrett, who records and gives solo concerts of total improvisation.

We have explained jazz at great length because it can provide some valuable experiences for young people. First of all, it can be an excellent training ground for composing, arranging and learning to improvise. Being involved in jazz forces the child to learn something about theory, chords and instrumentation. Learning gained from studying jazz can be applied to some contemporary music. For example, a teenager who had played a lot of jazz discovered that he could make the transition from jazz to the contemporary music of Alex Templeton's Pocket-sized Sonata for Clarinet with ease. Jazz notation and jazz chords were instantly understood by the youngster, whereas his classically trained teacher had to struggle to "translate" the music into the jazz idiom. Similarly, the boy found Aaron Copland's Concerto for Clarinet (originally written for Benny Goodman) simple to understand. After learning the concerto, this student should find the rest of Copland's music easy to play and to understand.

"Classical" Contemporary Music

Another avenue leading to the understanding and appreciation of contemporary music is the proper exposure at an early age. In this country, adults as audience or performers generally have had very little opportunity to acquire the aesthetic taste for contemporary music because American composers do not write for children. Most American composers tend to write "for each other"; they do not feel responsible for educating the young. Bach, Beethoven, Schubert, Bartok and Stravinsky (to name a few of the really important composers) all wrote for children. Today,very few composers bother to do this. If some of our major composers would or could write music for our youngsters, the children would learn how to deal with the new musical vocabulary and sounds as adult performers and audiences.

One of the authors recalls, "There are no words in which I can describe to you how difficult it was for me to learn and study Schoenberg's piano music - not because of lack of interest or ability, but mainly because none of my classical background prepared me for a manuscript that looked like that. Today Schoenberg Op. 19 sounds and reads clearly to me; it has become a standard repertoire for my young pupils.

I envy my students who are so much more musically learned than I was at their age. I am grateful that I bought that Stravinsky record as a child. Although I did not know how the page looked nor did I understand what Stravinsky was doing, I did learn to love the new sounds."

During the last ten years there has been some ground work done and we are in better shape than we were then. But there is much more that can be done. In the case of Massachusetts we are fortunate to have performance organizations such as Collage,Musica Viva, and the Fromm Concerts at Tanglewood whose sole intent is the presentation of new music. In terms of children's music, the Music School at Rivers in Weston has instituted a Contemporary Music Center for the Young. It is our hope that major composers will want to write good music for the young. At the same time, we have many teachers who find it difficult to present new music to their students. We suspect they don't know new music and have not kept up with their own studies. Music should be a living art and a music teacher should not retire after graduation, relying on his own old repertoire of music for the rest of his life. The teacher must keep abreast of what's happening in the field of music.

Presenting contemporary music to students can cause problems. One music teacher who presented new music to her students found that the parents were the ones who resisted the invasion of Bartok into their living room! Teachers should assign all students a contemporary piece plus several other pieces in different styles and periods to create a balance in the music studied. The teacher should assume responsibility for the musical education of the child by talking occasionally with the parents, explaining the choice of materials and their pedagogical values. It might sound surprising, but most parents find that their musical appetites have expanded due to the musical diet of their children. It is, after all, a matter of learning to recognize a sound, and there is no better way than hearing it many times.

To sum up, the enjoyment of some of the many forms and developments of music depends on one's musical background or exposure to music. One value of the popular forms of music is their instant acceptance and stimulus value to the young. The development of musical taste does not proceed in a straight line nor does it develop in some logical fashion. Instead, it broadens to include (or exclude) some or all forms of music as the listener or musician matures and changes.

CODA

coda.....a final or concluding passage,
which falls outside the composition, bringing it to a formal
close

Although we have written about and described many
different kinds of music for children, there are several issues in music education which we have not discussed.

In our view, music is a special means of communication, a universal language that touches all lives in
some fashion. The musical world is composed of three
important and interdependent parts: the creator or
the composer of the music, the performer or artist,and
the audience or listeners. In helping the children
learn music, we prepare them for a role in the music-
making process. Those children who have the appropriate abilities or gifts will become composers, others
with still a different set of gifts will become the
performers, and still others will take on the role of
the audience. The latter, who have neither the talent
nor the interest to dedicate themselves to a life in
music to the same degree as that of the composers or
performers, play a vital role in the world of music by
accepting, rejecting, living with and understanding
the music presented. Adults who were exposed to good
music as children and are knowledgeable about music
become superior audiences, demanding a high quality of
music and performance.

Because the attitude of the American federal government and the States has been one of "laissez faire"
toward music education, we do not have a strong national policy nor do we provide adequate funding and subsidy for the arts. This puts the responsibility for
music training squarely on the shoulders of the parents

and to a lesser extent on the public school systems.

The position of the public school systems on music education varies regionally. Some systems do an adequate job of music education while others consider it a frill, doing very little. A child growing up in the Midwest some 35 years ago progressed through a graded elementary program which, though not particular inspiring, did teach the reading of music. Contrasted with this experience is that of children currently educated in public school systems where music is taught only by rote. Those children deciding to play an instrument are the only ones who are given optional instruction and taught to read notes.

This view of music education contrasts with the situation in East Germany where a new Early Training in Music Program was started recently. Those children whose parents express an interest in having their children learn music (the children must exhibit talent when tested) are admitted to the Program. Classes are set at different levels of difficulty and take place after school hours. Children are regularly assessed for progress. In addition to private instrumental lessons, these children learn music theory and participate in ensembles and orchestras. By the time a talented child has reached the age of 12, he can transfer to a special school for even more intensive training.

Similar to the training in East Germany is the Russian music education system for children. It includes 5000 schools offering special music instruction and 30 special schools attached to Conservatories which provide the most intensive training for young people. One of the best of the 30 special schools is the Central Music School.

The Central Music School enrolls about 350 students taught by 100 teachers, most of whom are professors at the Moscow Conservatory. All students have two private lessons per week, group lessons in theory and other courses in music each day. The school day is divided with half a day devoted to music and the other half devoted to traditional school subjects. Children at the school manage to practice about 6 hours a day. Of the 40 children who were admitted in one particular year, most of the children had already decided what particular instrument they wanted to study and more than half had decided to study the piano. This contrasts with the situation in the United States where a child is not encouraged to make decisions about his future at an early age. In Russia, children grow up in an environment that encourages them to look beyond their own gratification to the needs and expectations of the greater society. A musically gifted child is considered an important asset of the Russian State...he is encouraged, nurtured and supported. Artists are treated with special respect and revered as national heroes. The main drawback - and it is a large one - is that the artist must conform to the expectations of the government - in his personal life, his artistic development, and in the opinions he expresses.

The Russian system has the advantage of providing training for anyone who merits it, regardless of financial circumstances. The authorities allocate funds for music on a scale reserved for Russia's most important projects. In a conversation, Milton Salkind, President of the San Francisco Conservatory, told one of the authors about his visit to a special music school where he witnessed pre-college level examinations. He commented on the fact that at different levels of talent, child after child performed without making mistakes, without producing a single ugly sound.

Of course, Russian governmental support has its price: the artistic standards and development are dictated by the government. However, the scope and the wealth of technique provided for the young at the expense of the government are outstanding.

There are some places in the United States, mainly in the big cities, where there are special high schools of performing arts, providing special training for gifted children. But there is no nationwide policy or across the board support for the arts. In the United States,we have funding through both the National Endowment for the Arts and Humanities and through State Arts Councils. The funding for the artists and musicians is limited to the mature and professional artist. For young children, most funding - which is limited - goes to Community Arts Organizations to bring the arts to groups who ordinarily would not be exposed to them. This contrasts with the policies of both East Germany and Russia as. well as other European countries which set aside a portion of their national budgets for arts funding and for development of the special talents of the young.

Since there is no single leader with a philosophy of music education in the United States (such as Kabalevsky in Russia, Suzuki in Japan, Kodaly in Hungary), increased financial support could be given to several of the different kinds of music institutions already in existence which can influence and direct the teaching of music to the young: Community Music Schools and the preparatory Departments of Conservatories.

Community Music Schools and Arts Centers have been the active cores of culture and have initiated a number of the most innovative programs in the arts as well as in community service. They have served cities and towns not only with fine teaching, but with a real sensitivity to the needs of the communities that they serve. Preparatory schools (schools under the umbrella of larger institutions such as Conservatories) should take responsibility for the special task of shaping the future artists by striving to identify and train the gifted and talented. Instead, they have been sidetracked by feeling threatened by the competition of Universities which have added music departments. All institutions are caught in the financial squeeze of spiraling inflation and thus compete against each other for funds. We believe that there is a definite role that each institution could play, thus allowing them to cooperate and survive the financial crunch.

Universities should deal with real music education programs with a goal of improving the public school music departments musically, socially and politically. Without a real commitment to the quality and importance of music in the arts and in the lives of the young in the public schools, the arts in the United States will go on fighting an endless battle.

Also, the University should be dealing with doctoral programs in musicology, research, and the diffusion of scientific and psychological discoveries and how they affect music; universities are equipped and staffed to deal with these areas. Research should become a priority and should deal with such topics as Accoustics, Electronic Music, Music Therapy, Pedagogy, Music History, etc.

Conservatories should deal with performance at its highest level, but only for the most promising young artists. The Preparatory Schools should deal with the teaching and shaping of the gifted young at the time when they may be the future Conservatory students. At present, most Preparatory Schools are stepchildren of the mother institution, extension divisions or moneymakers for the parent college. Two exceptions are the Juilliard School in New York and the Curtis Institute in Philadelphia, both of which have special schools devoted to the motivated and talented child.

Community Music and Art Centers should deal with sowing the seeds of a better life with art. Their role, along with that of the public school systems, is the most challenging and exciting: an intimate involvement with the community served, answering the needs of the community through arts, developing intelligent citizens and audiences and helping individuals channel their energy and talents. It is also important to note that the Community Music Center can fill another need, depending on the community in which it is located. Sometimes, because the school is located far from cities or Conservatories, the Music School must assume the role of a mini-Conservatory.

* * * * * * * *

While we have stressed that music is a tool of communication, a language and a vital part of life that everyone should have, we have not talked about the value of the process of learning music itself.

One of the assets to be gained through music lessons is the acquired discipline of how to learn. The majority of music lessons take place in a one-to-one situation (a very rare commodity these days.) The private lesson is individualized so that each student goes as fast or as slow as his ability and interests allow; therefore, gaining the confidence that comes with the solid understanding of the principles and content of music.

The writing of this book is the result of many conversations about what makes music lessons successful. We hope that this book is helpful to parents, by providing information to them so that the choices they make enhance their children's music lessons as an enriching experience not only to the child, but also to the family and society.

We strongly feel that the increased freedom of our times has had an unsettling effect of casting too many of our young people adrift in a sea of too many choices without much guidance. Rather than letting our children turn to drugs or drifting or alcohol, the learning of music and the other arts offers positive, stimulating, creative and attractive alternatives. It is clear that our inspiration comes from a deep love of the art of music and our experiences with all kinds of children whose lives were touched by music. That contact with music had a special meaning for every child - different for each, and positive for all.

BIBLIOGRAPHY

Apel, Willi & Daniel, Ralph, The Harvard Brief Dictionary of Music, Harvard U., Mass. 1960

Bailey,Philip, They Can Make Music, Oxford U. Press, New York, 1973

Brower,Harriette, Modern Masters of the Keyboard,1960 (reprinted by Arno Press, New York)

Cross, Milton & Ewen, David, The Milton Cross Encyclopedia of the Great Composers and Their Music, Vols. I & II. Doubleday, N. Y. 1953

Diller, Angela, The Splendor of Music, Schirmer, N.Y., 1957 (out of print)

Edwards, Ruth, The Compleat Music Teacher, Geron - X Los Altos, California 1970

Ewen, David, Famous Instrumentalists, Dodd Mead, 1965

Fisher, Renee, Musical Prodigies, Masters at an Early Age, Association Press, New York, 1973

Gell, Heather, Music, Movement and the Young Child, Australian Publishing Co., Sydney, 1949

Kodály, Zoltan, Selected Writings, Boosey & Hawkes, 1974

Landeck, B., Children and Music, William Sloane, 1952

Last, Joan, The Young Pianist, Oxford U. Press, New York, 1954

Markel, Roberta, Parents' and Teachers' Guide to Music Education, MacMillan, New York, 1972

Mills, Vera G. and Manners, Ande, A Parent's Guide to Music Lessons, Harper & Row, New York 1967

Montessori, Maria, The Discovery of the Child, Ballantine, New York, 1972

Morgenstern, Sam, Composers on Music; An Anthology Greenwood, (reprint of 1956 edition)

Pleasants, Henry, Serious Music and all that Jazz, Simon and Schuster, New York, 1960

Rubinstein, Arthur, My Young Years, Knopf, 1973

Schönberg, Harold, C. The Great Pianists from Mozart to the Present, Simon & Schuster, 1963

Shuter, Rosamund, The Psychology of Music Ability, Methuen and Co.,(Dist. thru Barnes and Noble) 1960

Slenczynska, Ruth & Biancolli, Louis, Forbidden Childhood, Doubleday, 1957

Suzuki, Shinichi, Nurtured by Love: A New Approach to Education, Exposition, 1969

Vinton, John, ed., Dictionary of Contemporary Music, Dutton and Co., Inc. New York, 1974

Wadsworth, Barry, Piaget's Theory of Cognitive Development, David McKay, New York 1971

A LIST OF RECORDINGS RECOMMENDED
FOR YOUNG PEOPLE

Bach:	Unaccompanied Cello Sonatas; Magnificat; Brandenburg Concertos
Beethoven:	Fifth Symphony; Ninth Symphony(last mov.)
Bizet:	Children's Games; Selections from Carmen
Britten:	Young Person's Guide to the Orchestra; Noye's Fludde; Ceremony of Carols
Chavez:	Toccata for Percussion
Copland:	Rodeo; Lincoln Portrait; Billy the Kid; Old American Songs
Debussy:	Children's Corner Suite
Dukas:	Sorcerer's Apprentice
Dvořák:	Slavonic Dances
Gershwin:	Rhapsody in Blue; American in Paris
Grieg:	Peer Gynt Suite; Piano Concerto
Handel:	Hallelujah Chorus
Haydn:	Surprise Symphony (2nd movement) Trumpet Concerto
Holst:	The Planets
Humperdinck:	Hansel and Gretel
Kodály:	Hary Janos Suite
Mendelssohn:	Piano Concertos, E minor Violin Concerto
Menotti:	Amahl and the Night Visitors
Mozart:	The Magic Flute; Bastien et Bastienne; A Musical Joke; Eine Kleine Nachtmusik; Clarinet Concerto; Flute and Harp Concerto
Mussorgsky:	Pictures at an Exhibition
Orff:	Carmina Burana
Poulenc:	The Story of Babar
Prokofieff:	Peter and the Wolf
Ravel:	Bolero; Mother Goose Suite; L'Enfant et les Sortileges
Respighi:	Fountains of Rome; Pines of Rome
Rimsky Korsakov:	Scheherezade
Rossini:	Overtures
Saint-Saëns:	Carnival of the Animals
Schuman:	Scenes from Childhood
Stravinsky:	Rites of Spring; Petrouchka
Tchaikovsky:	Nutcracker Suite; Sleeping Beauty; Swan Lake; Violin Concerto; Piano Con. No. 1

Vaughan Williams: Fantasia on Greensleeves
Verdi: Selections from Aida and La Traviata
Vivaldi: The Seasons

Folk and Children's Recordings

Theodore Bikel: For Children
Richard Dyer-Bennett: Songs with Young People in Mind
Tom Glazer (with Tripp): Songs to Learn by
Burl Ives: Best for Boys and Girls
Danny Kaye: Tubby the Tuba / Hans Christian Anderson;
             Songs for Children
Frank Luther: Babar, Songs and Stories; Winnie the
              Pooh & Christopher Robin; Funny Animal
              Stories; Favorite Children's Songs
Peter Seeger: Abiyoyo;
              Birds, Beasts, Bugs & Little Fishes
Peggy Seeger: Animal Folk Songs for Children
Russian Folk Songs for Children, (Petry)
Negro Folk Songs (sung by Leadbelly)
Israeli Children's Songs (Ben Ezra)
Jewish Children's Songs and Games, (Rubin, Seeger)
German Children's Folk Songs, (Vopel, Wolff)
French Children's Songs
Hola! Vamos a Cantar
Children's Marching Songs
Puff the Magic Dragon
Disney Favorites

(For the above listed recordings and others, check the
Schwann Children's Catalogue.)

The Staff - Music is written on a staff which is made up of 5 lines and 4 spaces

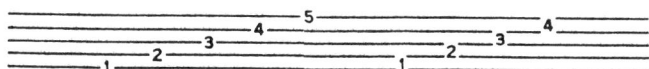

Notes are written on the lines and in the spaces of the staff, indicating the pitch

Bar Lines - The staff is divided into measures by bar lines

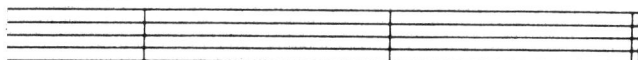

A double bar is placed at the end of the piece

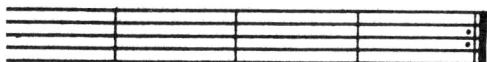

Two dots at the double bar mean to repeat

Clef Signs - A clef is placed at the beginning of each staff. It indicates the position of one note or pitch

Treble clef
or
g clef

Bass clef
or
f clef

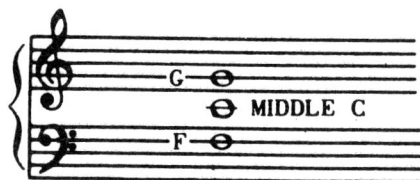

position of clefs
in grand staff

Pitches of Scale - in the Western modern scale the pitches are:

A   B   C   D   E   F   G
and the corresponding French syllables are:
La Si Do Re Mi Fa Sol

Duration of Notes and Corresponding Rests:

𝅝   Whole (4 counts)   ▬

𝅗𝅥   Half (2 counts)   ▬

♩   Quarter (1 count)   𝄽

♪   Eighth (1/2 count)   𝄾

♪   Sixteenth (1/4 count)   𝄿

Time Signatures - consists of two numbers. The number on the top tells how many counts (or beats) in a measure. The number on the bottom tells us what kind of note receives one count or beat

Example:

There are two counts in the measure and the quarter note gets one count

𝄴 - common time-4 beats to a measure 4/4

𝄵 - cut time, (alla breve) - 2 beats to a measure

- tie. Play and hold the first note for its indicated duration plus the time value of the note to which it is tied.

The Dotted Note:

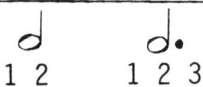

𝅗𝅥   𝅗𝅥.
1 2   1 2 3

When a note has a dot to the right of it, the dot increases its value by one half of itself

The Triplet:

A triplet is a group of 3 equal notes played in the time of 2 notes

126

<u>Accidentals:</u>		Symbols printed before a note; they raise or lower the note by one-half step
sharp	♯	play the closest note up the scale
flat	♭	play the closest note down the scale
natural	♮	cancels the note's previous alteration
double sharp	𝄪	raises the note by two half-steps
double flat	♭♭	lowers the note by two half-steps

<u>Key Signatures</u>

a group of flats or sharps at the beginning of a staff which tells which notes will be sharp or flat throughout the piece

<u>Other Symbols:</u>

𝄢.	press pedal (for the piano)
✲	release pedal (for the piano)
'	take a breath at this point
𝄐	fermata - hold the note, or pause if the sign refers to a rest

DICTIONARY OF MUSICAL TERMS

accel. (accelerando)	becoming faster
Adagio	slowly
Allegro	quick tempo
Allegretto	not as fast as Allegro
Andante	a walking pace; moderately slow
Andantino	slightly faster
Animato	animated
a tempo	resume the original tempo
cantabile	singing
Coda	ending or concluding passage
con	with
cresc.(crescendo)	growing louder
decresc.(decrescendo)	growing softer
D.C. (Da Capo)	go back to the beginning
D.C. al Fine	repeat from the beginning to the Fine
dim. (diminuendo)	getting softer
dolce	sweetly
D.S. al Fine	repeat from the sign (𝄋) to the Fine
D.S. (Dal Segno)	go back to the sign (𝄋)
espress. (espressivo)	with feeling, expression
Fine	the end
forte	loud
fortissimo	very loud
Giocoso	with humor
Grazioso	gracefully
Largo	very slowly
legato	connecting notes smoothly
Lento	slowly
loco	return to the normal note location

128

Maestoso	majestically
Marcia	march
meno	less
mf (mezzo-forte)	moderately loud
Moderato	moderately
molto	much
mp (mezzo piano)	moderately soft
mosso	motion, animated
non	not
p (piano)	soft
pp (pianissimo)	very soft
piu	more
poco	a little
poco a poco	gradually
portato	slightly disconnected
Presto	very fast
Prestissimo	faster than presto
rall. (ralletando)	gradually slowing
rit. (ritardando)	gradually becoming slower
riten. (ritenuto)	immediately slowing
scherzando	playfully
sempre	always
sfz (sforzando)	sudden emphasis on a note or chord
simile	continue in a similar manner
sostenuto	sustained
stacc. (staccato)	detached notes
troppo (ma non)	not too much
Vivace	lively
Vivo	alive, brisk

AN INTRODUCTION TO THE DISCIPLINE OF MUSICAL NOTATION

The purpose of this project was to demonstrate how children can learn and understand the use of universal symbols for musical communication.This particular project was used with two groups of children;gifted five-year olds and a group of 2nd and 3rd graders.The teacher's role was to encourage,guide,and amplify the children's ideas which the teacher then wrote on the blackboard.

The children were asked to suggest a story which has a beginning, some events or action,and an ending. After agreeing on the structure of the narrative,the events were written on the blackboard and divided by bar lines:

1) a walk in the woods	2) beautiful singing bird	3) a tiger	4) attacks bird
5) thunder stops tiger	6) bird flies away	7) rain	8) run home	9) bird sings again

Now, the children improvised sounds and actions to represent the events of the story:

1) tap rhythm with feet; whistle bird sounds	2) solo whistle trills;song-like	3) heavy thumps and roars
4) roars and whistles	5) crashing sound made by voice	6) silent, winglike motions
7) long shhh sound by voice	8) fast thumping made by feet	9) solo whistle trills,song-like

130

The next step was to define the events by prescribing dynamics and phrasing:

1) mp
   andante

2) (music notation TR. with phrase mark)

3) (music notation < > with barline)

4)   f-ff

5) FFF

6) (fermata notation)

7) p

8) gliss.

9) (music notation TR. with phrase mark) ‖

The final step is to translate the sound effects into instrumental sounds through improvisation on an instrument. (In this particular case, it was the piano).The teacher writes the improvisation on the blackboard to show how it looks in actual musical notation.The score then becomes a "map" for the children's performance.

⊔ = white key cluster with left hand palm

ABOUT THE AUTHORS

A. RAMÓN RIVERA, who was born in Puerto Rico, studied music with Sanroma. A graduate of the New England Conservatory of Music, Mr. Rivera served as Director of the N. E. C. Preparatory Department and is now Chairman of the Piano Department at the Music School at Rivers in Weston, Massachusetts, where he co-founded the Center for Contemporary Music for the Young.

For almost 20 years Mr. Rivera has taught piano to hundreds of students, including many winners of performance and composition awards and soloists with the Boston Pops Orchestra.

Mr. Rivera received fellowships to Tanglewood and Castle Hill, has performed with the Boston Pops Orchestra, at the Gardner Museum, Berkshire Music Festival, television and has performed extensively in Puerto Rico. An Arts Program Advisor to WGBH-TV, Mr. Rivera has served on the Massachusetts Council for the Arts and the Board of the National Guild Of Community Schools of Music.

THELMA GRUENBAUM comes from the Midwest and is a graduate of the University Of Chicago with degrees in the Liberal Arts and Human Development. She taught Nursery School and was a Psychology instructor at the Home Study Department at the U. of C. At Yale University she served as a research assistant in the Psychology and Social Sciences departments.

A resident of Massachusetts since 1961, she was Manager of a Youth Chamber Orchestra and is Manager of DAPELE, her sons' Trio which recently recorded its first record album, Bop 'n Pop and all that Jazz.

Mrs. Gruenbaum's published writings include a series of articles on mental health and Before 1776, a children's book on colonial days in Massachusetts. Future projects include a book of short stories, Snapshots, Frames and Short Exposures and a children's book on the Holocaust in collaboration with her husband.